ISLAMIC FUNDAMENTALISM

KAZENGA P. TIBENDERANA received his doctorate in African history from the University of Ibadan, Nigeria, under a Rockefeller Foundation sponsorship in 1974 after completing undergraduate work in history at Makerere University College of the University of East Africa. He is currently a professor of African history in the Department of History at Makerere University, where he teaches African history and Development Studies. Professor Tibenderana worked for Ahmadu Bello University, Zaria, as a Senior Research Fellow (1978-83), concentrating on Traditional and Islamic Education Systems in Nigeria, and as a Senior Lecturer and then Reader in African History (1984-88). In addition to doing research at the University of Wisconsin - Madison (1992 - 93), as part of the prestigious Fulbright international exchange of scholars programme, Professor Tibenderana has held a visiting appointment at the Islamic University in Uganda (2002-2003). His research has been published in such diverse scholarly journals as *The Journal of the Historical Society of Nigeria, The Journal of African History, The African Studies Review,* and *The Journal of African Studies.* He is the author of *Education and Cultural Change in Northern Nigeria 1906 - 1966: A Study in the Creation of a Dependent Culture* (2003) and *Sokoto Province under British Rule* 1903-1939 (1988). Professor Tibenderana was Head of the Department of History at Makerere University from 1994 to 2001, and a member of the Makerere University Council from 1997 to 2001. He is currently (2005) a member of the University Council of Kampala International University and Chairman of its Appointments, Promotions and Disciplinary Committee. He is also a member of the Kabale University Appointments Committee. He specialises in the history of Islamic societies in West Africa and the growth and development of Islam there. And, though born into a Christian family, Professor Tibenderana has assimilated the Islamic culture and fully appreciates it. He is married with four grown-up children.

Islamic Fundamentalism

The Quest for the Rights of Muslims in Uganda

Kazenga P. Tibenderana

FOUNTAIN PUBLISHERS
Kampala

Fountain Publishers
P.O. Box 488
Kampala
Tel: 256-(41)259163/251112 Fax: 251160
E-mail: fountain@starcom.co.ug

Distributed in Europe, North America and Australia by African Books Collective Ltd. (ABC), Unit 13, Kings Meadow Oxford OX2 0DP, United Kingdom. Tel: 44-(0) 1865-726686, Fax:44-(0)1865-793298

© Kazenga P. Tibenderana 2006
First published 2006

All rights reserved. No part of this publication may be reprinted or reproduced or utilised in any form or by any means, electronic, mechanical or other means now known or hereafter invented, including copying and recording, or in any information storage or retrieval system, without permission in writing from the publishers.

Qur'anic quotations in this book are taken from The Holy Qur'an: English Translation of the meanings and commentary, King Fahd Holy Qur'an Printing Complex.

ISBN-13: 978-970-02-572-5
ISBN-10: 9970-02-572-4

Dedication

This book is dedicated to my Nigerian Muslim friends who welcomed me into their communities and homes with open arms and generous hospitality, and for giving me easy access to the Islamic culture. And to the memory of my teacher and friend, Professor Abdullahi Smith, for his brilliant intellect, and for his academic excellence.

Contents

Abbreviations	x
Glossary	xi
Foreword	xvii
Preface	xx
Acknowledgements	xxv

1. **Introduction** — 1
   - A Global Revival of Religion — 1
   - The Muslim Community in Uganda — 5
   - Methods of Data Collection — 10
   - Sampling Procedure — 13

2. **Towards Understanding Islam** — 15
   - The Doctrines — 15
   - Islamic Political Thought: Fundamentalism — 20

3. **Conceptualisation of an Islamic State** — 27
   - The Islamic State and the *Shura* — 27
   - Islam and Politics — 30

4. **Religio-political Rights of Muslims under an Islamic State** — 38
   - An Introductory Comment — 38
   - The Right to be Ruled by a Fellow Muslim — 40
   - The Right to be Ruled in Accordance with the Sharia — 41
   - The Right to Say the Five Canonical Prayers and to Attend the *Jumu'a* Prayer — 42
   - The Right to Fast during the Ramadhan — 45
   - The Right to go on the Hajj — 46
   - The Right to Wage a Jihad of the Sword — 49
   - The Right to Pay *Zakat* — 54
   - The Right to Acquire Education — 57

The Right to Marry Four Wives and to Divorce by
Repudiation   61
The Right to Marry Four Wives   61
The Right to Divorce by Repudiation   62

5. **Ugandan Muslims' Perception of the Rights
   of Muslims**   68
   An Introductory Comment   68
   The Right to be Ruled by a Fellow Muslim   68
   The Right to be Ruled in Accordance with the Sharia   69
   The Right to Say the Five Canonical Prayers and to
   Attend the *Jumu'a* Prayer   71
   The Right to Wage a Jihad of the Sword   73
   The Right to Pay *Zakat*   74
   The Right to Acquire Education   77
   The Legacy of Colonial Education   80
   The Right to Marry Four Wives and to Divorce by
   Repudiation   85
   Conditions for Muslim Marriage   85
   The Foundations of Islamic Legislation   87
   Muslim Marriage under Threat   88

6. **From Timidity to Self-assertiveness**   95
   The Islamic Resurgence   95
   Futile Attempts at Forming an Islamic Political Party   98
   Opposition to Political Parties   106
   Contestation over Muslim Voters' Votes in Future
   National Elections   111
   Foreign Involvement in the Clamour for the Rights
   of Muslims   113
   The Containment of Islamic Populism   117

7. Which Way Forward?	120
Conclusions and Policy Suggestions	120
Conclusions	120
Policy Suggestions	122
Bibliography	128
Index	135

Abbreviations

DP	Democratic Party
FIS	Islamic Salvation Front
IPK	Islamic Party of Kenya
NGOs	Non-Governmental Organisations
NRM	National Resistance Movement
OIC	Organisation of Islamic Conference
UIRP	Uganda Islamic Revolutionary Party
UMSC	Uganda Muslim Supreme Council
UMYA	Uganda Muslim Youth Assembly
UPC	Uganda People's Congress
UPDF	Uganda People's Defence Forces

Glossary

Arabic terms occurring in the text

Al-jihad al-akbar: the greater jihad

Al-jihad al-asghar: the lesser jihad

Allah: the proper name of God in Arabic. The word Allah has no plural and no feminine gender

dar al-harb: the realm of war or non-Muslim territory.

dar al-Islam: the realm of Islam or the territory of Islam.

da'wa (also spelt as da'awa): propagation of, or call to Islam.

dhimmi: a non-Muslim living under the protection of Muslim rule. He has the right to practise his religion in return for recognising Islamic law, Muslim authority, and for paying *jizya*. (For the meaning of *jizya* see below.)

fatwa: a formal legal opinion, given by an official or unofficial mufti, i.e. a person appointed, or at least competent, to give such opinions. The request for such an opinion may be made by a *Qadi* (Muslim judge of sharia) or by the State, or by a private individual; and on the basis thereof the *Qadi* may decide a case or the individual order his behaviour.

fitra: instinct, innate or natural disposition.

Hadith: the authentic record of Prophet Muhammad's words, sayings, and actions and his acceptance of the actions done by others in his presence without comment on them.

hajj: the greater pilgrimage to Mecca which takes place in the last month of the Islamic calender (lunar year). In Uganda the term is used as a title before the name of any Muslim male who has returned from the greater pilgrimage.

hakimiyya: divine governance.

Hanafis: the followers of the largest of the four Sunni schools of law which mutually recognise each other as orthodox. The Hanafiya is by far the most widespread and numerous of all Sunni schools of law: it was adopted by the Ottoman Turks as their official school and thus represents that of the courts, if not always of the population, in Egypt, the Sudan, Palestine, Syria, Iraq, while it is also the dominant school in Central Asia and India.

Hanbalis: the followers of the smallest of the four orthodox schools of law, they are largely limited today to the Wahhabis of Arabia. Strictly speaking, however, the Wahhabis are regarded as having put themselves outside the confines of orthodox Islam, for they have repudiated the authoritative Hanbali tenets on a number of points. Instead, they are enthusiastic supporters of the teachings of the two Hanbali reformers, Ibu Tiymiya and Ibu al-Qayyim.

Id-al-Adhha: The Id-al-Adhha is a four-day festival at the end of hajj. The '*id* of the (greater) sacrifice, it starts on the 10th day of *Zul-hijjah* (the month of hajj). It is the day on which the pilgrims sacrifice their animals.

Id al-Fitr: A three-day festival after the month of fasting Ramadhan).

iddat: a period after divorce or the death of her husband for which a woman waits before remarrying to ensure that there is no confusion about the paternity of children.

ihram: a pilgrim garb. A simple garment of unsewn cloth in two pieces which pilgrims must wear from specific points on their approach to the holy city of Mecca.

ijma: Consensus or agreement. The orthodox view is that this constitutes a valid source of law for, although an individual jurist may err in his deductions from the sacred texts, the community as a whole is infallible. Much difference of opinion has prevailed, however, as to what in fact constitutes *ijma*. Some limit it to the agreement of the companions of the Prophet; some to the consensus of the whole Muslim people; but most regard it as adequately fulfilled, if the leading jurists of any age are in express or implied (presumed) agreement.

ijtihad: literally, to exercise personal judgement. The practice of reasoning in order to interpret the sharia.

imam: a Muslim prayer-leader; also in certain contexts 'head of the Islamic state', equivalent of khalifa. In addition it is used by some, and especially the Shi'is, for the leader of the whole Muslim community, whom the Shi'is insist must have been divinely designated and who they regard as impeccable and infallible.
Islam: literally, to submit. The religion of all the Prophets of Allah, including Jesus (Isa) son of Mary, confirmed and sealed finally by the mission of the Prophet Muhammad.
jahili: paganist societies.
jahiliyyah: materialistic paganism.
jihad: the exertion or struggle including war against evil or unbelief. In the case of pagans they were to be given the choice between Islam and the sword, while the 'people of the Book', i.e. Jews and Christians, were to be given the further alternative of submission, tribute and protection.
jizya: a protection tax imposed on non-Muslims under the protection of Muslim rule.
Jumu'a: the day of gathering, Friday, and in particular the *Jumu'a* prayer.
Khalifatullah: Allah's viceroy on earth.
khutba: sermon usually given during *Jumu'a* prayer.
Malikis: the followers of the school of law which grew up in the Hijaz and subsequently adopted Malik ibn Anas as their nominal founder. One of those four Sunni schools which mutually recognise each other's orthodoxy. The Maliki school preponderates in Sudan, Upper Egypt and throughout North Africa, while in West Africa, it is virtually unrivalled.
mahr: The mandatory marriage gift (i.e. dowry) which is given to a bride by the bridegroom at the time of their marriage.
masjid: place of prostration, i.e. mosque.
muezzin: one who calls Muslims to prayer.
mufti: Muslim jurist competent to give formal legal opinions on matters of legal interpretation and to issue a ruling (*fatwa*); or a leader of a Muslim community, as in Uganda.

mujahidun (also spelt as mujaheddin): participants in a jihad.
Muslim: one who professes the faith of Islam or who is born to Muslim parents.
Qadi: Muslim judge appointed by the state, or the UMSC in the case of Uganda, with administrative as well as judicial duties.
Qur'an: the final revelation given to the Prophet Muhammad in Arabic. Ethymologically the term Qur'an simply means 'reading'; theologically it means the word of Allah incarnate. It is eternal and uncreated. The Arabic copy that a Muslim uses today is an exact replica of a heavenly prototype, dictated word by word to the Prophet Muhammad through the Angel Gabriel (Jibril).
Ramadhan: The ninth month of the Islamic calender during which Muslims fast.
sadaqa: a gift made to obtain a heavenly reward and it cannot be revoked.
Shafi'is: Those who adhere to the school founded by al-Shafi'i. Like the Hanafis, Malikis and Hanbalis, the Shafi'is represent one of the four 'orthodox' schools of law. It is predominant in Lower Egypt, East Africa, much of Arabia, the Red Sea Littoral, and throughout South East Asia.
Sharia: Islamic law.
Shawwal: the tenth month of the Muslim calender.
sheikh (also spelt as shaikh): a head of a town or an Arab tribe. In Uganda it is used to mean a learned and respected Muslim.
Shi'is: originally used of the sect of Ali. The term now covers a number of different sects, all of which are regarded by the four Sunni (orthodox) schools as heterodox and all of which similarly regard the Sunnis as in error. In reality, however, the sub-sects of the Shi'a are of very different degrees of 'heterodoxy' as is well recognised by Sunnis today.
shura: consultation. Radicals view *shura* not merely as a religious doctrine but also as public will and, ultimately, the divine will. The modern *shura*, as advocated by al-Banna and

others, postulates the necessity of people's involvement not only in political matters but also in all issues concerning the community. *Shura* denies the legitimacy of authoritarian rule or political monopoly over the community and makes the community the source of executive power.

Sunna: the tradition based on the Qur'an and on the acts and sayings of the Prophet Muhammad which governs the practice of Sunni Islam.

Sunni: One who follows the Sunna or traditions of the Prophet, a member of the largest Muslim group, which is commonly termed orthodox. Sunni Muslims follow one of four main schools of law: Hanafi, Hanbali, Maliki and Shafi'is.

surah: a chapter of the Qur'an.

tabliq: to convey the message of Islam to the public, i.e. to propagate Islam. Locally, *tabliq* refers to an Islamist movement otherwise known as *salaf* with its headquarters at Nakasero and Market Square mosques.

talaq: repudiation, or divorce. This is allowed to all Muslims upon the unilateral decision of the husband, although it is commonly regarded as sinful to divorce one's wife without good cause. When done only once or twice the divorce is revocable. If, however, the divorce is for the third time, it is not only immediately final but the parties are also precluded from remarriage unless or until the wife has undergone an intervening marriage.

taqiyya: pretended acquiescence.

tawhid: belief in the Oneness of Allah.

ulama: those with religious knowledge, commonly those who have completed a course at a *madrasa* (school or college for Islamic religious studies).

Ummah: literally, a nation but is usually applied to the Muslim Brotherhood.

umrah: a less formal pilgrimage to Mecca at any time of the year.

zakat: a wealth tax. It is one of the indispensable pillars of Islam.

Zul-hijjah: the month of Pilgrimage. It is the twelfth month of the Muslim calendar.

Zul-qa'da: the eleventh month of the Muslim calendar.

Foreword

In spite of having reached Uganda three decades (1840s) before the arrival of Christianity (1870s), Islam in Uganda still remains a minority religion. Rather, it is Christianity that is now a dominant religion in the country. Today, in terms of numbers, as shown in this book, Muslims constitute the third largest religious group after Catholics and Protestants.

Of course, many reasons have been advanced to explain Islam's failure so far to capture more converts than Christianity despite the fact that it reached Uganda much earlier than Christianity. These reasons include the following, among others:

1. Islam was introduced by Muslim traders and not missionaries. And for these traders the spread of Islam was a secondary occupation to their preoccupation, i.e., trade, in Uganda. It is thus argued that in its early days Islam did not spread to all parts of Uganda, particularly those areas which lacked trade items that were sought after by traders from the East African coast.

2. When the Christian missionaries arrived in Uganda they adopted more systematic, aggressive, and efficient methods of spreading Christianity. As a result, the argument goes, they were able to counteract the spread of Islam and even to undo some of the gains that Islam had made before the arrival of Christian missionaries in Uganda. Also, the Christian missionaries had ample financial resources from their benefactors in Europe to build numerous churches, schools and hospitals while all that Muslims could afford were a few mosques.

3. The policies of the British colonial administration in Uganda (1900 – 1962) strongly favoured the spread of Christianity at the expense of Islam. In this regard, the British colonial rulers helped Christian missionaries in various ways to establish schools and

build churches and hospitals in many different parts of Uganda, thus accelerating the spread of Christianity in the country.

Whatever reason or reasons one may accept for Islam's slow progress in Uganda, the truth of the matter is that by 1900 Muslims had been defeated in a civil war in Buganda Kingdom by their Christian foes. They were subsequently relegated to the third class position in Kiganda society, after the Protestants and Catholics. Indeed, while under the terms of the Anglo-Buganda Agreement of 1900 Christian churches were allocated 92 square miles (148 sq. km.) of land, no land was allocated to Muslim institutions! Moreover, through defeat in the civil war, Muslims lost political power in Buganda and were hardly represented in the new political structures of the colonial state.

Given the above trend of events, there is small wonder, then, that at the time of Uganda's independence in October 1962, it was the Christian Ugandans who inherited state power from the British colonial rulers. This power bestowed on the Christians the right to distribute the 'national cake'. Indeed, there were only two (2) Muslim university graduates in the entire country in 1962. Muslims had only one secondary school compared with 26 for Catholics and 10 for Protestants. And, while the welfare of the Muslim population has slightly improved since independence, Muslims still lag far behind Christians in many sectors of Ugandan society. The number of Muslims in top positions in the state bureaucracy and in the Cabinet is so small that it does not reflect the size of the Muslim population in the country, for example. Currently, out of 30 Permanent Secretaries, only one is a Muslim, while out of 66 ministers only four are Muslim.

Under these circumstances many of the Muslims' religio-political rights have so far been ignored. Professor Tibenderana highlights some of these rights in the present book. *Islamic Fundamentalism: The Quest for the Rights of Muslims in Uganda* is well researched and in many different ways gives a synopsis of the situation of Muslims in Uganda. He draws on his wealth of experience about Muslims and their rights in Nigeria where he taught and lived for about 14 years.

In spite of his Christian background, Professor Tibenderana has tried his very best to write the present book from a neutral position. And, while the book may contain some arguments with which one may not agree, nonetheless, it fills a vacuum in our knowledge of the Muslims' religio-political rights in Uganda. It helps the reader to appreciate some of the odds which Muslims in Uganda have had to battle against, and continue to grapple with, in order to keep the banner of Islam raised in Uganda.

I strongly recommend the book to all those who wish to widen their knowledge of Islam and Muslims' religio-political rights in Uganda.

Dr Ahmad K. Sengendo, Ph.D (Kansas)
Rector, Islamic University in Uganda
25 October, 2005
22nd Ramadhan, 1426 A.H.

Preface

It is not uncommon these days to hear Imams deliver incendiary sermons condemning the Movement government for adopting anti-Islam laws or policies, and prodding their audiences 'to fight for their rights'. But rarely, if ever, do these Imams, or other Muslim leaders for that matter, spell out quite clearly what constitutes the rights of Muslims in Uganda. Consequently, the audiences are often left bewildered by the Imams' exhortations for Muslims 'to fight for their rights' since many Muslims in Uganda are not well acquainted with these rights. The chief aim of this book, therefore, is to provide the background information necessary for the understanding of the rights of Muslims, both as they exist in orthodox Islam, and as they are understood and practised in Uganda. In a world where the inter-religious relations grow ever more complex, we need constantly to deepen and refine our understanding. This little book is an innovative way of addressing this need by making accessible vital information, which otherwise would be out of reach to the general reader. It provides a dimension that widens to good effect the scope of studying Islamic principles and practices.

We live in a globalised world, where local events can have an international impact. Fundamentalism, as a powerful contemporary and future political and social movement, is neither limited to, nor predominant in, only one country or region. It is on the rise all over the world. Within the emerging new world order, religion is likely to play a major role in regional and international politics, whether it manifests itself in fundamentalist mass movements or in dynamic features of world civilisations. Hence, constructions of modernisation, secularisation, and rationalisation are giving way to trends of post-modernisation, religionisation, and spiritualisation.

We are also already witnessing the growing weakness of the world's nation-states and the rise of constructs based on concepts of religion and civilisation inspiring the emergence of regional entities. The threat to the nation-states also emanates from various social forces.

But, while some of these social forces, such as ethnic formations, demand decentralisation, autonomy, and independence, those based on religion, particularly Islam, and civilisational formations, demand increased centralisation, unity, and interdependence.

The nature of conflict can also be expected to change in the international arena, and as such social forces gain ground by becoming either more localised, as in the case of ethnic formations, or more universalised, as in the case of religious and civilisational formations. This calls for an understanding of the phenomenon of Islamic fundamentalism on the part of the citizens of the world's nation-states, including the citizenry of Uganda, whether they are Muslim or not. Only then can the conflicts that are bound to arise from competing claims of the localised agendas and universalised agendas be minimised. It is for this very reason that the present book includes a discussion on Islamic fundamentalism. Also, brief discussions on the global revival of religion and Islamic Resurgence are provided to give the current Islamic Resurgence in Uganda a world-wide perspective.

Islam still remains 'the misunderstood religion' in many circles among the general reading public in the country today. It is commonly believed by most Christians in the country, for example, that a Muslim man can divorce his wife or wives at will. Of course, implicit in this outrageous belief is the impression that marriage in Islam is a temporary bond, unlike in the Christian religion which continues to adhere to the 'till-death-do-us-part' doctrine even in cases where the marriage is long dead! The book argues that, although divorce is permitted for Muslims, nevertheless, marriage in Islam is meant for life and divorce is very much frowned upon in Muslim communities.

Also, in the heat of Miss Amina Lawal's trial and conviction for committing adultery by a sharia court in Nigeria, which sentenced her to death by stoning in August 2002, His Eminence Emmanuel Cardinal Wamala, Archbishop of Kampala, Uganda, condemned Lawal's conviction and called for the abrogation of the specific law under which she was charged and convicted, describing it as 'a bad law and unfair', adding that 'sharia law can be wrong' (*The New Vision*, August 27, 2002:4). This audacious criticism, coming as it did from the head of the Catholic Church in the country, further attests to the claim that Islam still remains 'the misunderstood religion' to wide circles among the general reading public in Uganda, since His Eminence ought to have known that Miss Lawal was fairly convicted in accordance with Islamic criminal law (Peters 2003:19-21) and that the sharia or Islamic law cannot be abrogated by man. It also shows utter lack of respect for Muslims' sensitivities on the part of the Cardinal.

If we are to continue to live in harmony in this multi-cultural, multi-ethnic and multi-religious country, and to develop a functional democracy, then the Christians and Muslims among us should endeavour to understand and appreciate each other's religious beliefs and practices. This is the only way we can minimise religious conflicts in future. For, as the Qur'an says, 'ignorance is the source of vice'. For example, in the aftermath of Pentagon's admission in June 2005 that on five different occasions during 2002 – April 2005 US soldiers at Guantanamo Bay in Cuba desecrated the Qur'an, honest observers of the US military aptly imputed this unwarranted and sacrilegious behaviour to the soldiers' unfamiliarity with Islam. Thus it is most likely that had the US soldiers been familiar with Islam, and had they been appreciative of the sacredness of the Qur'an and the fact that every Muslim treats it with great reverence, they would not have wantonly desecrated it. The world could then have been spared the rioting that erupted in some Muslim countries, e.g. Pakistan and Bangladesh, when the international media broke the news of 'mishandling the Qur'an', to borrow Brig.-Gen. Jay Hood's phraseology, by US soldiers at Guantanamo Bay. (Brig.-Gen. Hood was the Guantanamo Bay commander at the time of the incident.) Moreover, if Uganda's policy-makers are to develop policies that are sensitive to Muslims' beliefs and practices, they should have a sound knowledge of the rights of Muslims. Policy-makers need to know, for instance, the things that are forbidden to Muslims, e.g.

the consumption of alcohol, and to contrive policies and schemes for making it possible for Muslims to fulfil their religious obligations without necessarily trampling on the rights of non-Muslims.

The present book introduces the rights of Muslims to those unfamiliar with Islam and gives them guidance with Qur'anic quotations. The emphasis is on presenting information in a readily retrievable form. The extensive glossary enhances retrievability of information. It is put at the beginning of the book, rather than at the end, as is usually the case, because for most readers in Uganda, particularly non-Muslim ones, it is indispensable for the understanding of the text.

In a book which tries to cover the rights of Muslims that are as old as Islam itself, it is obviously not possible for one to claim originality in terms of either source-material or interpretation. My sources, to put it bluntly, are secondary, and I have cited them in the text for use by students as references for further study. For interpretation, I have, on the other hand, depended on the opinions of established authorities in the field of Islamic sciences of traditions and sacred law. It has been my primary aim to make the issues raised in this book easily accessible to readers in Uganda rather than to answer questions on problems pertaining to the rights of Muslims in a secular state such as Uganda.

Of course, the conclusions reached in this book are only tentative, since they are based on a small sample. Their main purpose, therefore, is simply to stimulate interest in the students of Islam to carry out a more comprehensive research on a wider subject, i.e. the co-existence between the Muslim minority and the Christian majority in a modern, democratic, and secular state, such as Uganda, so that they can provide conclusive answers to the questions that the present book either totally ignored or attempted only superficially. This little book should be regarded as fuel for thought! It will appeal to the clergy and other religious leaders; political office-holders and aspirants to political office; activists for gender equality; civil society leaders; legal practitioners; education administrators; teachers and students, especially those in Islamic-oriented colleges; and men and women of good will who wish to understand the new trends in the quest for the rights of Muslims and the upsurge in political Islam all over the world; and who have the desire to protect freedom of worship and to promote religious co-existence in our country.

Let me say a word or two to non-Muslim readers, particularly Christians, who tend to equate the Bible with the Qur'an. In order to appreciate, and perhaps understand fully, what is written in this book, one should sincerely accept the fact that Muslims truly believe that the Qur'an is the word of God incarnate, infallible, and, that it is the only Book through which God speaks directly to mankind. This belief is basic and fundamental to the Muslims' way of life. It is not required, however, that one should share this belief with the Muslims. All that is required of a non-Muslim reader is to have an 'imaginative understanding' of the ideas behind Islamic thought and the Muslims' actions.

Also, the true meaning of some of the Qur'anic quotations in this book are hard to grasp unless one has a fair knowledge of the text in which the quoted verse or verses occur. Thus, in a way they are quoted out of context. Therefore, they should be read with great caution to avoid unintended misconceptions and imputing untruths on the part of the author.

That this book does not question the validity of the beliefs it deals with is a well-judged decision for which the author offers no apology. For to have done otherwise would have meant writing an entirely different book. The author feels least qualified to write such a book, however.

My dear reader, if after reading this little book you feel the desire to read more about Islam, my effort in writing it will have been worthwhile. And if you find anything in this book disagreeable to you, please let it not spoil your enjoyment of the rest of the book. Good reading.

Kazenga P. Tibenderana
KAMPALA, 2005

Acknowledgements

Several individuals and institutions provided invaluable support during the process of writing this book. It is with much pleasure and gratitude that I acknowledge the help and advice of Professor Mahdi Adamu, the former Rector of the Islamic University in Uganda, (IUIU), who provided me with some Islamic texts that were not easily accessible to me. Many scholars read varying portions of the book at different stages of development. Each offered a unique perspective that was ultimately woven into the final fabric. I am particularly indebted to Dr Ahmad Kawesa Sengendo, the Rector of the Islamic University in Uganda, who read the manuscript in its entirety and offered invaluable suggestions for revision; and who in addition wrote the Foreword to this book. I also owe a debt of gratitude to Dr Anas Abdunoor Kaliisa, the Vice Rector of the same university, for his meticulous reading of the manuscript, as well as for his helpful and incisive criticisms and suggestions which have saved me from many errors and infelicities. An intellectual debt is due to Hon. Justice Dr G.W. Kanyeihamba, who read the manuscript in its entirety and gave me the benefit of his experience, particularly as a writer on Ugandan affairs, including the politics of Islam. I particularly wish to thank Dr Hannington Sengendo, Dean Faculty of Arts, for his constant encouragement. I am also extremely grateful to Dr Abasi Kiyimba, the Deputy Dean of the Faculty of Arts, Makerere University, and Chairman of the UMYA, who kindly provided thoughtful critiques of the earlier versions of Chapters 5 and 6. I wish also to record my gratitude to Haji Edris Kasenene, the Secretary-General, UMSC, for his advice with regard to Chapter 7. I wish to acknowledge my great debt to Mr Blaze Babigumira of Babigumira & Co. Advocates for providing me with some documents which were out of my reach and, of course, for his encouragement and moral support. I am also extremely grateful to my son, Dr Charles T. Tibenderana, for his moral support and for supplying some vital documents which were unknown to me. I take this opportunity to record my huge indebtedness posthumously to the late Professor Abdullahi Smith whose association during the early years of my academic career has meant more to me than can be expressed here. He not only taught me the meaning of 'true friendship' but also initiated me into the study of Islamic civilisation and culture with a sympathy and encouragement that will be ever cherished.

Several institutions also made generous contributions during the writing process.

Grateful acknowledgement is made to Makerere University for granting me sabbatical leave during 2002-2003 from my academic duties in which to write the book. My particular gratitude is also due to the IUIU for offering me temporary employment during my sabbatical leave, and to the academic staff of the same university who welcomed me into their community with the most generous and unique friendship, and in whose congenial and stimulating company my ideas were nourished, tested, and refined. In particular I would like to thank Dr Sowed Mayanja of the Faculty of Law, and Mr Ssuna S. Ndaula of the Faculty of Islamic Studies, both of whom have answered my inquiries on the specific points, or, more generally, discussed with me matters treated in this book.

This book has also greatly benefited from the intellectual exchanges with my own Muslim students at Ahmadu Bello University, Zaria, Nigeria (1983-88), at Makerere University (1990-2002), and at the IUIU (2002-2003). It is through the trial and error of teaching Islamic civilisation and culture to undergraduate students that I have been able to sharpen my arguments and focus on those topics of greatest importance. I am most grateful to all of them. I especially would like to thank my research assistants who helped me to collect oral data, namely Sule Abubakar, Harshim Mwenyi, Sulaiman Kafeero, Yusuf Kasumba, Muhammad Sekatawa, Aisha Nakawooya, and Farouk Makumbi. They performed their assignment with much enthusiasm and with punctilious attention.

Acknowledgement xxvii

I am glad of an opportunity to thank my lifelong friend, Hon. Professor Tarsis B. Kabwegyere, Minister of Local Government, for his unfailing moral support and for providing the daily encouragement necessary for such a long-term project. I am also extremely grateful to the many public servants and politicians, particularly Lt. Gen. Elly Tumwine of the UPDF; Maj. Gen. F. Okecho of the UPDF; Dr Ahmed Kisule, Uganda's Ambassador to the Islamic Republic of Iran; Maj. Gen. Ivan Koreta, the Commandant of the Senior Military Staff College, Kimaka, and Dr Sam Nahamya, Permanent Secretary, Ministry of Trade and Industry, who have readily discussed with me many aspects of the Muslim factor in Uganda. Above all, but for the stimulating discussion I had with Hon. Amama Mbabazi, Minister of Defence, in 2001, this book might never have been written. I owe a debt of gratitude to him for his subtle prodding questions on the new trends in the radicalisation of Islam in Uganda.

I also appreciate the assistance given to me by the staff of Sir Kashim Ibrahim Library of Ahmadu Bello University, Nigeria; the Centre for Basic Research, Kampala; the Makerere University Main Library, and the University Library of the IUIU, where I got most of my written sources. I am particularly grateful to Josephine Sanyu Namugwanya of the History Department, Makerere University, who has typed and retyped successive drafts of the manuscript with a minimum of fuss and a maximum of intelligence and with unfailing cheerfulness. I would like to thank my sister, Mrs Jane Mary Tushemereirwe, who has sacrificed much of her time to attend to our parents while I was busy writing the book. I am particularly indebted to my brother, Mr Paul Kasozi Kazenga, for the special encouragement he gave me. I particularly wish to thank the editorial and production staff at who Fountain Publishers Ltd., and the copy editor, expertly polished and transformed my manuscript into a book.

I wrote this book on the insistence of my wife, Keinywanisa, who, despite many disappointments, continues to entertain a world of illusion about my academic abilities. I remain grateful for her unbounded kindness and ever-gentle guidance.

To all those whom I have mentioned, as well as to others whom I have no space to name, I am most sincerely grateful. None of the people I consulted, of course, has the slightest responsibility for the contents of this book. This is my exclusive responsibility.

K. P. T.

1

Introduction

A Global Revival of Religion

It is important to open our discussion with a comment on the dramatic global revival of religion that has been unfolding since the 1970s. It is very much hoped that a knowledge of this phenomenon will facilitate our understanding and appreciation of the factors which have led to the Islamic resurgence in the world in general and in Uganda in particular.

In the first half of the twentieth century intellectual elites, especially in the West, generally assumed that economic and social modernisation was leading to the withering away of religion as a significant element in human existence. This assumption was shared by both those who welcomed and those who deplored this trend. Modernising secularists hailed the extent to which science, rationalism, and pragmatism were eliminating the superstitions, myths, irrationalities, and rituals that formed the core of existing religions. The emerging society would be tolerant, rational, pragmatic, progressive, humanistic, and secular. Worried conservatives, on the other hand, warned of the dire consequences of the disappearance of religions, beliefs, religious institutions, and the moral guidance religion provided for individual and collective human behaviour. The end result would be anarchy, depravity, and the undermining of civilised life.

But, as S.P. Huntington tells us (Huntington, 1996:96), the second half of the twentieth century proved these hopes and fears unfounded. Economic and social modernisation became global in scope, and at the same time a global revival of religion occurred. This revival has pervaded every continent, every civilisation, and virtually every country. In the mid-1970s the trend towards secularisation and the accommodation of religion with secularism was discarded. A new religious approach took shape, aimed no longer at adapting to secular values but at recovering a sacred foundation for the organisation of society by changing society if necessary. Expressed in a multitude of ways, this approach advocated moving on from a modernism that had failed, attributing its setbacks and dead ends to separation from God. The theme was no longer modernising but a 'second evangelisation of Europe', the aim was no longer to modernise Islam but to 'Islamise modernity'.

This religious resurgence involved people returning to, reinvigorating, and giving new meaning to the traditional religions of their communities. Islam, Christianity, Hinduism, Buddhism, orthodoxy, all experienced new surges in commitment, relevance, and practice by erstwhile casual believers. In all of them arose fundamentalist movements committed to the militant purification of religious doctrines and institutions and the reshaping of personal, social, and public behaviour in accordance with religious tenets. However, the fundamentalist movements are only the surface waves of the much broader and more fundamental religious tide that is giving a different cast to human life at the end of the twentieth century. In many societies the renewal of religion manifests itself in the daily lives and work of people and concerns and projects of governments.

The most obvious, most salient, and most powerful cause of the global religious resurgence, according to Huntington (Huntington, 1996: 97), is precisely what was supposed to cause the death of religion: the process of social, economic, and cultural modernisation that swept across the world in the second half of the twentieth century. Long-standing sources of identity and systems of authority are disrupted. People move from the countryside into the city, become separated from their roots, and take up new jobs or no job. They interact with large numbers of strangers and are exposed to new sets of relationships. They need new sources of identity, new forms of stable community, and new sets of moral precepts to provide them with a sense of meaning and purpose. Religion, both mainstream and fundamentalist, meets these needs.

Throughout history in the Muslim world there has been a recurring tendency, in times of emergency, for Muslims to find their basic identity and loyalty in the religious community, that is to say, in an entity defined by Islam rather than by ethnic or territorial criteria. Thus re-Islamisation from below is first and foremost a way of rebuilding an identity in a world that has lost its meaning and become amorphous and alienating. And, as shown in Chapter 2, fundamentalist movements are a way of coping with the experience of chaos, loss of identity, meaning and secure social structures created by the rapid introduction of modern social and political patterns, secularism of the Western Model, scientific culture and economic development.

More broadly, the religious resurgence throughout the world is a reaction against Westernisation, moral relativism, and self-indulgence, and a reaffirmation of the values of order, discipline, work, mutual help, and human solidarity. Religious groups meet social needs left unattended by state bureaucracies. The breakdown of order and of civil society creates vacuums which are filled by religious, often fundamentalist, groups.

The collapse of communism in the former Soviet Union, its severe modification in China, and the failure of socialist economies to achieve sustained development have now created an ideological vacuum. People see communism as only the latest secular model to have failed, and in the absence of compelling new secular deities they turn with relief and passion to the real thing. Religion takes over from ideology, and religious nationalism replaces secular nationalism.

The movements for religious revival are anti-secular of the Western Model, and, except in their Christian manifestation, anti-Westernisation. They also are opposed to the relativism, egotism, and consumerism that is associated with 'modernism' as distinct from 'modernity'. By and large they do not reject urbanisation, industrialisation, development, capitalism, science, and technology, and what these imply for the organisation of society. In this sense they are not anti-modern. 'Religion is the motor of development', and according to Dr Hassan al-Turabi (cited in Huntington, 1996: 100), 'a purified Islam will play a role in the contemporary era comparable to that of the Protestant ethic in the history of the West. Nor is religion incompatible with the development of a modern state'. Thus the movements for religious revival accept modernisation and the inevitability of science and technology and the change in the lifestyles they bring, but they are unreceptive to the idea that they be Westernised.

Participants in the religious resurgence come from all walks of life but overwhelmingly from two constituencies, both urban and both mobile. Recent migrants to the cities generally need emotional, social, and material support and guidance, which religious groups provide more than any other source. The other principal constituency is the new middle class embodying the 'second-generation indigenisation phenomenon' – the revolt against the West by non-Western peoples originally legitimated by asserting the universality of Western values; it is now legitimated by asserting the superiority of non-Western values. In both former European colonies and independent countries like China and Japan the first 'moderniser' or post-independence generation often received its training in Western universities in a Western cosmopolitan language. Partly because they first go abroad as impressionable teenagers, their absorption of Western values and lifestyles may well be profound. But not so with most of the much larger second generation who, in contrast, gets its education at home in universities created by the first generation, and the local rather than the colonial language is increasingly used for instruction. These universities provide a much more diluted contact with the metropolitan world and culture, and knowledge is indigenised. The graduates of these universities resent the dominance of the earlier Western-trained generation and hence often succumb to the appeals of nativist opposition movements. As Western influence recedes, young aspiring leaders cannot look to the West to provide them with power and wealth. They have to find the means of success within their own society, and hence they have to accommodate the values and culture of that society.

The activists in Islamic fundamentalist movements are not the aging conservatives or illiterate peasants but people who are modern-oriented, well-educated, and pursue careers in the professions, government, and commerce. Among Muslims, particularly in the Arab world and Southeast Asia, the young are religious, their parents secular. Much the same is the case with Hinduism, where the leaders of revivalist movements again come from the indigenised second generation and are often successful businessmen and administrators.

Religion, indigenous or imported, provides meaning and direction for the rising elites in modernising societies. More than anything else (Marty and Appleby, 1993:569), reaffirmation of Islam, whatever its specific sectarian form, means the repudiation of European and American influence upon local society, politics, and morals. In this sense the revival of non-Western religions is the most powerful manifestation of anti-Westernism in non-Western societies. That revival is not a rejection of modernity; it is a rejection of Westernisation, Western Model secularism, and relativistic, degenerate culture associated with the West. It is a declaration (Huntington, 1996:101) of cultural independence from the West, a proud statement that: 'We will be modern but won't be you'.

The Muslim Community in Uganda

Islam was first introduced in Uganda by Arab and Swahili traders from the East African coast during the 1840s. Since then to-date (Kasozi, 1986), it has made slow but steady progress punctuated by short spells of rapid growth. The 1959 Uganda Population Census (Kasozi, 1986:7) put the country's total population at 6.4 million people. Of these, 34.5% were Roman Catholics, 28.2% were Protestants while 5.6% (or 204,000 people) were Muslims. The Uganda Population Censuses of 1969 and 1980, did not give the religious affiliations of the country's population. However, according to the 1991 Uganda Census (Uganda Government, 1995: 64) Uganda had a population of 16.7 million people. The religious composition of this population was 7.4 million or 45% Catholic; 6.5 million or 39% Anglican; 1.8 million or 11% Muslim; with the rest being made up of smaller Christian denominations and non-Christian. Also, the 2002 Uganda Population Census (Uganda Bureau of Statistics, 2005:11) showed that of Uganda's population of 24.4 million people, 10 million or 42% were Catholics; 8.8 million or 36% were Anglicans; 3 million or 12% were Muslims while the rest were made up of smaller Christian denominations and non-Christians.

However, the number of the Muslim population (3 million) computed in the 2002 Uganda Population Census is hotly disputed by Muslim leaders who believe, rightly or wrongly, that the number of Muslims in the country is much higher 'than the Government is willing to admit'. From their point of view the methods so far used to enumerate the Muslim population in previous censuses were too deficient in accuracy to produce reliable results. There is little doubt however that the Muslim population in Uganda today (2005), which recorded a percentage increase of 1.6% during 1991-2002, is well over 3 million people. But in the absence of reliable statistical data regarding the religious composition of Uganda's population, we can conjecture that the Muslim population in the country today constitutes a large minority. And, judging from the growth rate recorded by each religious denomination during 1991-2002 (Uganda Bureau of Statistics, 2005:11), Islam is the fastest growing religion in Uganda today.

A good number of Uganda's Muslims today are first generation Muslims, that is, their parents are not Muslim. Islam has had a short history in the country. And, as Dr Kasozi rightly observes (Kasozi, 1986:4), Islam 'has not yet been truly and entirely woven into the social fabric of those who believe in it. It does not influence every aspect of the lives of those who practise it, as is the case on the coast of East Africa'. Islam penetrated Uganda piecemeal, in that there was no wholesale forced conversion of whole ethnic groups, as was the case in West Africa, for example. Thus, apart from Islam being the religion of a minority, Muslims do not live in a conterminous territory that would give them a sense of an Islamic political community. Rather, they are widely dispersed throughout the country, and live in small pockets sandwiched between Christian majorities. They are not evenly distributed throughout the country, however.

By 1959 (Kasozi, 1986:5), 41.7% of Uganda's Muslims lived in Buganda, 38.2% lived in the Eastern Region, 14.7% lived in the Northern Region, and 3.4% lived in the Western Region. This pattern of the dispersion of the Muslim population remains unchanged despite the fact that the number of Muslims in Uganda has significantly increased since 1959. In Uganda, Islam is a religion of urban dwellers, thus reflecting the way it was introduced in the country. It was in towns that Muslim traders who brought Islam to Uganda settled and carried out their commercial activities. However, there are pockets of Muslim concentration in certain rural areas. In Buganda, for example, the British colonial rulers allocated Butambala county to the Muslims in 1892. Again (Kasozi, 1986:8), many of the descendants of the former Sudanese troops who were Muslim live in Aringa county in West Nile, which is said to have a population that is 80% Muslim. Also, Bugwere county in Busoga, and Arua, Yumbe and Koboko counties in West Nile region, have a high concentration of Muslims. In Ankole, Muslims are found mainly in Bukanga and Shema where early Muslim Baganda refugees settled.

Until very recently, Islam in Uganda developed slowly and in isolation from the influences in the older Muslim world, i.e. the Middle East. The Muslim community in Uganda neither sent students to foreign Islamic colleges and universities nor received clerics or men of letters from such institutions on training tours, at any rate, up to the 1970s. And to make matters worse, Islamic education in Uganda was neglected by her colonial rulers (1900 – 1962) and their immediate Ugandan successors (1962-1970) with the result that the existing Qur'anic schools and colleges in the country were few in number and offered very poor quality education as many of them still do today. Of course, until the establishment of the Islamic University in Uganda (IUIU) in February 1988, Uganda did not have an institution for higher Islamic education. Speaking generally, Muslims in Uganda tend to be less educated in Islamic studies than their co-religionists, say in Tanzania or Kenya, who have had a very long association with Islamic scholarship in the Middle East. Indeed, Dr Kasozi, (Kasozi 1986:118), himself a Muslim, has partly imputed the failure of the Muslim leaders to institutionalise the Uganda Muslim Supreme Council (UMSC), especially during the 1970s and early 1980s, to 'the lack of an educated leadership'. He argued, for example, that many of the leaders of the UMSC during the period were mere graduates of Qur'an schools, 'who are not qualified to tackle the diverse problems of the modern [Islamic] world'.

But things are changing for the better. Since Idi Amin's rule (1971-79) many deserving Ugandan Muslim youths have secured scholarships annually from Arab states, especially Saudi Arabia, Sudan, and Libya, to pursue diploma and degree courses mainly in Islamic studies in the colleges and universities in the sponsoring country. However, this internationalisation of the training of Uganda's potential imams and sheikhs is not entirely innocuous. Graduates of foreign colleges and universities who have returned to the country after the completion of their courses of study are largely blamed for stirring up the religious diversities and doctrinal disagreements that currently exist among Uganda's Muslims. As a matter of course, Uganda Muslim youths who studied in foreign Islamic institutions are routinely exposed to and influenced by various Islamic theological schools of thought prevailing in the colleges or universities they attend. And, when they return to Uganda, they become ardent proponents of their newly acquired doctrines and practices regardless of whether or not these doctrines and practices are generally accepted by Muslims in Uganda.

Thus, Ugandan youths who have returned to the country from Saudi Arabia, Kuwait, and other Gulf states after completing their courses of study, and who obviously were exposed to the

Salafi doctrines, are said to be largely responsible for heightening the doctrinal contentions between the Ugandan Sunni Muslims who adhere to the Sufi doctrines and those who adhere to the Salafi doctrines. For, whereas most Sunni Muslims in Uganda are adherents of the Sufi doctrines, the graduates of the colleges and universities in the Middle East and Gulf States, where the Salafi doctrines preponderate, usually adopt the Salafi doctrines on their return to Uganda with a high sense of self-assurance and contempt for their local doctrinal adversaries.

Theologically, the Muslim population in Uganda is not homogeneous. Rather, it is divided into various sects, i.e. the Sunni, the Shia, the Islamailis and the Ahmadiya. The Sunni sect is by far the largest and the most widespread in the country while the Ahmadiya sect is undoubtedly the smallest of the four sects. Moreover, the Sunni sect constitutes the main stream of Islam in Uganda and in the world at large. The great majority of Uganda's Sunni Muslims are more or less closely attached to the Sufi Order. There are also, of course, quite a number of Sunni Muslims in the country who conform far more closely and generally to the dictates of the Salafi Order. This group, as noted above, is largely made up of graduates of foreign colleges and universities, particularly those in Saudi Arabia, Kuwait and other Gulf states where the Salafi Order preponderates. The exact number of these graduates is not known, however. Neither the government nor the UMSC keeps up-to-date and accurate records of the Ugandan Muslim youths who each year travel abroad to pursue courses in higher Islamic education in colleges and universities in foreign Muslim countries. Uganda's Muslims, like other minority groups in the country, often complain of being marginalised by the Movement government, especially in terms of political appointments, recruitment into lucrative posts in the state bureaucracy, and the award of government business contracts and scholarships.

But the Muslim population in Uganda, many of whom, three decades ago, could not dare to openly use their Muslim names for fear of being victimised, especially if they attended Christian founded schools and colleges or if they sought jobs in the state bureaucracy, have since acquired a high degree of self-confidence, to the extent that today they constitute the boldest and most vocal group in the country in clamouring for the rights of interest groups, i.e. the rights of Muslims. Muslims' fear of victimisation by colonial authorities on the basis of their faith was well founded. It should be recalled, for instance, that the ultimate objective of Christian mission schools and colleges was to proselytise for Christianity (see, e.g., Tiberondwa, 1998), and that the colonial administration gave preferential treatment to Christian candidates in its employment policy.

Thanks to Idi Amin's administration (1971-1979), which bestowed upon Muslims such overwhelming favours in commerce and government employment by way of contracts and appointments to the state bureaucracy, thereby elevating them from their previous obscure socio-political position into prominence. (On the favours which Idi Amin's regime bestowed upon the Muslim community see, e.g., Kasumba, 1995: 129-144; and Kayunga, 1994: 333-335.) Indeed Idi Amin's regime accelerated the boosting of the Muslim's self-esteem and group identity. This, in turn, galvanised the Muslim population into strongly demanding the observance of the religio-political rights of Muslims. Moreover, since Idi Amin's rule (1971-79), the Muslim population in Uganda has been growing very rapidly, partly as a result of the favourable policies implemented by successive governments since then, and partly as a result of the assistance and material support it has so far received from foreign-based Muslim Non-Governmental Organisations (NGOs) during the same period.

Of course, the assertiveness of the Muslim population in Uganda was also fuelled by the worldwide revival of religion, which perhaps reached the acme of its development during Idi Amin's rule (1971 – 1979). For, as shown above, it was truly a global phenomenon which affected, and still affects, each and every country in the world, including Uganda.

However, with the greater religious freedom ushered in by the National Resistance Movement (NRM) government in 1986, the differences between the sects have tended to widen. This has resulted in cut-throat competition between the sects for new converts. Each of the sects propagates its own brand of Islam and requires its clientele to strictly adhere to its approved religious beliefs and practices.

In the medium term, this development does not seem to pose serious political problems. However, in the long term, it is bound to produce a Muslim community that is so severely fractured internally that it will be ungovernable, since its demands on the government of the day would inevitably be too diverse and too divergent to be met. It is largely for this reason that governments in Muslim countries, like Egypt, Saudi Arabia, United Arab Emirates, Iran and Libya, have found it necessary to impose restrictions on the calibre of people who can disseminate religious knowledge, and on the religious literature that the public can access. In fact, the long-term objective of the founding fathers of the UMSC was, and perhaps still is, to create a more homogeneous Muslim population from the fractious groups in which it was divided prior to the establishment of the UMSC in June 1972. And, although doctrinal inter-sect differences might be more vigorously and bitterly contested today (see, e.g., Kanyeihamba, 1998) than they were before the inception of the UMSC – largely owing to increased Islamic scholarship – nonetheless, Muslims in the country are more united in purpose than they were in 1986 when the NRM captured state power. They are now better placed to engage in self-help projects to improve their welfare and to catch up with the Christians, particularly in the educational sector.

Methods of Data Collection

The research method adopted in the present study was both empirical, i.e. relying or based on factual information, observation or direct sense experience-usually as opposed to theoretical knowledge; and perceptual, i.e. relating to, or characterised by, physical sensation as conditioned by experience. It also relied on multiple data sources, e.g. questionnaire, interviews, and documentation. A combination of several data collection techniques was adopted in this study in order to generate both quantitative and qualitative data. A questionnaire was administered as the basic method of generating data, particularly that which might be quantifiable. The questionnaire, which contained 33 semi-structured questions, was directly administered to respondents who did not know enough English to understand the questions by six Muslim research assistants, each covering a designated area on a more or less face-to-face interview basis. Besides being Muslim, the research assistants are also fluent speakers of the vernacular languages of the respondents they interviewed. On the other hand, a pre-established questionnaire was used to collect data from respondents with sufficient knowledge of English to be able to comprehend the questions.

The questionnaire was delivered to the respondents in this category by the research assistants who later retrieved the responses. The 33 questions in the questionnaire were designed to collect the following types of data:

1. Biographical data including the social and educational backgrounds of the respondents.
2. Respondents' perception of the rights of Muslims.
3. Respondents' knowledge of Islam and its main institutions.
4. Respondents' attitude towards the present governance of Uganda.

A total of 70 copies of the questionnaire were completed by one of the two methods mentioned above and returned to the principal researcher. Data was collected during 1999 – 2000.

I also gleaned information from published works, e.g. books, academic articles, newspapers, and magazines. The use of multiple data sources, or triangulation, allowed me to address a broader range of attitudinal and observational issues. It was hoped that the use of more than one data-gathering technique would greatly strengthen the study's usefulness to other settings.

No approach depends solely on one method, any more than it would exclude a method merely because it is labelled 'quantitative', 'qualitative', 'case-study', 'action research', or whatever. Methods are selected because they will provide the data one requires to produce a complete piece of research. Decisions have to be made about which methods are best, for instruments must be designed to do the job. Since the main objective of my research was to understand the individuals' perception of the religio-political rights of Muslims, I found it imperative to adopt a qualitative approach, especially since my research sought insight rather than statistical analysis.

I also considered the case-study approach to be particularly appropriate for my kind of research since it would provide an opportunity for one aspect of a problem, in this case, the Muslims' perception of the religio-political rights of Muslims, to be studied in some depth within a limited time scale. As in all research, evidence was collected systematically, and the relationship between variables was studied. It was thought that the case-study approach would allow me to concentrate on the religio-political rights of Muslims and to identify, or attempt to identify, the various interactive processes at work. These processes may remain hidden in a large-scale survey and yet may be crucial to the success or failure of a political system.

Sampling Procedure

In this study the target population was the Muslim population. However, a member of this target population had to be a Sunni Muslim and a citizen of Uganda. Sunni Muslims were selected as the target group for this study owing to the fact that they constitute the main stream of orthodox Islam, not only in Uganda, but throughout the Muslim world, and to avoid being entangled in the doctrinal controversies that currently exist between different Muslim sects in the country. Owing to limited time and scant financial resources, the research subjects were selected from the districts of Kampala, Iganga, Luweero, Mbale, Masaka, Mpigi and Mukono. These districts were selected largely because their Muslim inhabitants regularly interact with foreign Muslim visitors and have easy access to both Western and Islamic education. The research subjects were selected on the basis of their sect, faith, level of educational attainments, geographical area, and whether they were male or female.

The sample or research subjects consisted of three categories. The first category comprised 40 people with formal Western education and perhaps with some Islamic education as well. The second category consisted of 10 people with some formal Islamic education. The third category consisted of 20 people with no formal education, whether Western or Islamic. These categories of people were deemed necessary to provide information necessary for the study. And, although 110 copies of the questionnaire were sent out, only 70 respondents (64%) either returned the questionnaire or engaged in face-to-face interview with the research assistants. The data collected from this sample was from a cross-section of only the Sunni Muslim population, however.

2

Towards Understanding Islam

The Doctrines

The intrinsic worth of the religio-political rights of Muslims, which is the subject of this study, cannot be appreciated without a fair amount of knowledge of the Islamic faith. And, although I cannot pretend to provide such knowledge in this short chapter, it is nevertheless, essential to briefly comment on the crucial terms in the Islamic faith which are quite pertinent to the present study. The information provided here is merely intended to make us appreciate the uniqueness of the religio-political rights of Muslims which makes these rights seem trivial and insupportable to a great majority of non-Muslims.

Islam (literally 'to submit') is the religion of all the Prophets of Allah (God) 'including Jesus (Isa)' confirmed finally by the mission of the Prophet Muhammad. Islam has three main aspects: religious, political and cultural. The three overlap and interact, sometimes imperceptibly passing from one to the other. Islam, the religion, is a system of beliefs and practices revealed by God to the Prophet Muhammad in the 7th century, enshrined in the Arabic Qur'an, complemented by the Sunna (practice and way of life of Prophet Muhammad).

Theologically, the Qur'an means the word of Allah incarnated. It is eternal and uncreated. The Arabic copy that a Muslim uses today is an exact replica of a heavenly prototype, dictated word by word, to the Prophet Muhammad through Angel Gabriel (Jibril). God speaks of the Qur'an (see Surah 5:16) as a root of spirit and life, and as a light by which the servants of God, i.e. Muslims, are guided to the straight path. God further speaks of the Qur'an (Surah 69:51) thus: 'But verily it is Truth of assured certainty', i.e. is infallible. 'This is the Book,' God further says (Surah 14:1), 'which we have revealed unto you, in order that you might lead mankind out of depths of darkness into light'. Thus, in all its dimensions, the Qur'anic wisdom is conclusive.

Islam, the state, is a political entity with an aggregate of institutions based on the sharia (Islamic law). The sharia, according to the traditional view, is eternal, universal, perfect, fit for all times in all places. It recognises no difference between the sacred and the secular. It sets forth and regulates man's relations with, and obligations to, God, as well as his relations with his fellow man. The sharia, or divine law, is not given by any earthly ruler or king. It always remains valid, whether or not it is recognised by the state. The sharia, in a technical sense, is the totality of God's commandments.

To the Muslims, the Qur'an, being the very word of God, is the authority wherefrom emanates the very conception of legality and every legal obligation. Among the Muslims, there is no doubt that the chief lawgiver is God. Every other legislating authority must base its legitimacy on revelation. Thus the sharia, in classical Islamic theory, is the revealed Will of God, a divinely ordained system preceding, not preceded by, the Islamic state, controlling, and not controlled by, the Muslim society.

But the institutionalised practice of *ijtihad* (legal interpretation) (Mamdani, 2004:60) allows for the interpretation of sharia to take into account changing historical circumstances and, therefore, different points of view. It makes for a substantive body of law constantly changing in response to changing conditions. The attitude towards *ijtihad* is the single most important issue that divides society-centred from state-centred—and progressive from reactionary–Islamists. And, whereas society-centred Islamists insist that the practice of *ijtihad* be central to modern Islamic society and call for *ijtihad* to be modernised and democratised so that the law could be interpreted by a body elected by the community of Muslims, and not the religious *ulama*, state-centred Islamists are determined that the 'gates of *ijtihad*' remain closed. State-centred Islamists are staunch defenders of the sharia, but they understand the law as divine and see any form of democracy as corruptive of it. Human beings must, individually and collectively, surrender all rights of overlordship, legislation and exercising of authority over others. No one should be allowed to pass orders or make commands in his own right and no one ought to accept the obligation to carry out such commands and obey such orders provided they are in consonant with the Islamic law. Indeed Muslims are commanded not to surrender to any one save God. The Qur'an says (Surah 7:3):

> Follow (O men!) the revelation
> Given unto you from your Lord,
> And follow not, as friends
> Or protectors, other than Him.
> Little it is ye remember
> Of admonition.

The Islamic concept of life, as envisaged in the Qur'an, is that man should devote his entire life to the cause of Allah. Indeed, every system of life is a religion, realising that a religion or system is the method that organises life. Conversely, religion should not be made up of abstract notions but should regulate life, in general, and discipline behaviour, in particular. The religion of an individual is his consistent behaviour. Thus those Muslims who do not make Islam their system of life are not truly Muslims. (A Muslim is one who professes the faith of Islam or who is born to Muslim parents.) They may have partially followed Islam (Moussalli, 1999: 134-35), but this is insufficient to make somebody a true Muslim, since mere belief without active adherence is worthless and is not conducive to good life. This applies to government, state, society, and political life as well as to the individual, the personal and so forth.

There are four 'orthodox' schools of the sharia. These are: Hanafis, Malikis, Hanbalis, and Shafi'is. The Shafi'is are predominant in Lower Egypt, East Africa, much of Arabia, the Red Sea littoral, and throughout Southeast Asia. The most distinctive feature of Malikis' and Hanafis' legal theory, as opposed to that of the Shafi'is and Hanbalis, is their recognition of supplementary sources of law. Suffice it to say here that the existence of the four 'orthodox' schools of law accounts for the varying interpretations of the sharia.

The other important term to consider here is the jihad which is casually uttered by radical Islamists. The term jihad means exertion or struggle, including war, for the purpose of doing God's Will. The jihad is a doctrine shared by all Muslims, and which is now hotly contested. The debate around radical political Islam is thus increasingly a debate on the meaning of the jihad. The jihad is part of the five pillars of Islam and is binding on every Muslim. The Qur'an insists (Mamdani, 2004:50) that a Muslim's first duty is to create a just and egalitarian society in which poor people are treated with respect. This demands a jihad on all fronts: spiritual and social, personal and political. Professor Mamdani tells us (Mamdani, 2004:50) that scholars of Islam distinguish between two broad traditions of jihad: *al-jihad al-akbar* (the greater jihad) and *al-jihad al-asghar* (the lesser jihad). The greater jihad, it is said, is a struggle against weaknesses of self, it is about how to live and attain piety in a contaminated world. Inwardly, it is about the effort of each Muslim to become a better human being. The lesser jihad, in contrast (Mamdani, 2004:50), is about self-preservation and self-defence; it is directed outwardly, and is the source of the Islamic notion of what Christians call a 'just war', rather than a holy war. Thus jihad is a doctrine of spiritual effort of which military action is only one possible manifestation. At the same time, political action is not contradictory to jihad. Islam sanctions rebellion against an unjust ruler, whether Muslim or not, and, as Mamdani observes (Mamdani, 2004:50), the lesser jihad can involve a mobilisation for that social and political struggle. The lesser jihad can be waged either through the tongue – by preaching – or through material and financial inducements, or by war. Its ultimate objective is to protect the interests of Islam. The lesser jihad or armed jihad or jihad of the sword can be waged against unbelievers as well as Muslims accused of half-heartedness or apostasy. The consensus among Muslim jurists is that Muslim rulers who obstruct the way of Islam and put wordly standards before Islam are heathens against whom armed jihad is legitimate. The jihad is obligatory on upright and conscientious Muslims.

However, Hasan al-Banna, one of the most well-known Islamic thinkers of the 20th century, argues (see Moussalli, 1999:61) that Islamic jihad is not a message of aggression and ambition but is sanctioned for the protection of *da'wa* (propagation of or call to Islam), as a guarantee for peace, and as a fulfilment of the divine mission of justice and right.

If the jihad, as traditional Islamic jurisprudence views it, is the exertion of utmost efforts, it requires long-term actions that include scientific, industrial, and spiritual preparations. From a fundamentalist perspective, all this necessitates, in turn, an intellectual and mental revolution. One of the founders of modern Islamic fundamentalist thought, Abu al-Hasan al-Nadawi, divides these preparations into, first, proper education about Islamic goals as opposed to *jahiliyya* (materialist paganism) so that no confusion is entertained, and, second, cultivation of the scientific and technological power necessary to fight the *jahiliyya*. He further argues (Moussalli, 1999:62) that old concepts must not be reconciled with Islamic ones but must be abolished altogether. In the place of old concepts and societies, Islamic ones should emerge in order to execute the sharia. Only by doing this can a Muslim society and an Islamic state emerge.

The jihad of the tongue (*daawa*) remains obligatory for Muslims until the whole world is converted to Islam.

Historically, the practice of the lesser jihad as central to a 'just struggle' has been occasional and isolated, marking points of crisis in Islamic history. After the first centuries of the creation of the Islamic states (Mamdani, 2004:51-53) there were only four widespread uses of the jihad as a mobilizing slogan – until the Afghjan jihad of the 1980s. (On these four jihads see, e.g., Mamdani, 2004:51-53.)

Islam, the culture, is a compound of varied elements – ancient Semitic, Indo-Persian, classical Greek-synthesised under the caliphate and expressed primarily through the medium of the Arabic tongue. Unlike the other two, Islam, the culture, was mainly formulated by conquered peoples, Arabicised and Islamised, rather than by Arabians. It holds the distinction (Hitti, 1970:3; and Abraham, 1989) of having been, from the mid-8th century to the end of the 12th century, unmatched in its brilliance and unsurpassed in its literacy, scientific and philosophical output.

Islamic Political Thought: Fundamentalism

Admittedly, the term 'Islamic fundamentalism' is very controversial indeed. Professor Mamdani cautions us, for example (Mamdani, 2004:36-37), that 'To speak of fundamentalist Islam, at least in the case of mainstream Sunni Islam, is misleading. He further argues that the problem with using the term 'fundamentalism' to describe all political movements that speak the language of religion is that it tends to equate movements forged in radically different historical and political contexts, and obscures their doctrinal differences, including the place of violence in religious doctrine. 'Religious fundamentalism', in Mamdani's view, 'is akin to a countercultural, not a political, movement'. Therefore, he asserts that 'fundamentalism', as a religious phenomenon, has to be distinguished from those political developments that are best described as political Christianity and political Islam. Thus, in Mamdani's view (Mamdani, 2004: 47), it makes more sense to speak of political Islam – the preferred designation in the Arab world for political movements that speak the language of religion – than of Islamic fundamentalism, the term most often used in post - 9/11 America.

But, whereas Professor Mamdani's arguments here are ingenious and academically sound and, while we need to take note of them, it is equally true that they are not persuasive enough to cause the term – Islamic fundamentalism – to fall into disuse immediately. Thus the term Islamic fundamentalism shall be adopted for this study to denote Islamic political movements aiming at essentially reviving, both politically and religiously, the fundamentals of Islam – the

Qur'an and the Sunna of the Prophet Muhammad – which function as the only authoritative texts in the formation of an Islamic state. Fundamentalism is a term that was developed in the West in order to describe the belief of some evangelists in the Bible as the literal and eternal word of God. Later this meaning was expanded to include all sorts of religious groups that attempt to live according to their revelations; thus, there is Jewish fundamentalism, Christian fundamentalism and Islamic fundamentalism. And, although fundamentalism has been loaded with negative connotations, it is employed here to describe the movement that calls for the return to the fundamentals of Islam – that is, the Holy Qur'an and the Sunna. Islamic fundamentalism, as opposed to other fundamentalisms, is politically revolutionary, not conservative. It is both a philosophy and a way of life that brings together politics and theology and makes the latter dependent on the former. (This definition is adapted from Moussali, 1999:17-18.) The adoption of the term Islamic fundamentalism in this book is in no way intended to portray Islam as a religion of extremism and violence. (On Islamic fundamentalism in Uganda see, e.g., Kayunga, 1994:319-363.)

Since Islam in Africa, Asia and the Middle East was debased by colonialism, and since there is urgent need to revive the fundamentals of Islam in these areas, it goes without saying that in the context of the definition we have adopted for Islamic fundamentalism, the mainstream Sunni Muslims are all fundamentalists since they must be in support of the revival of, both politically and religiously, the fundamentals of Islam. However, the onset of political Islam during the Cold War gave rise to movements with diverse, even contradictory political agendas. Moderate movements organise and agitate for social reform within the existing political context. Radical movements (Mamdani, 2004:38) organise to win state power, here and now, having concluded that the existing political situation is the main obstacle to social reform. There are two kinds of radical movements, society-centred and state-centred: whereas society-centred radical Islamists link the problem of democracy in society with the state, state-centred radical Islamists pose the problem of the state at the expense of democracy in society.

Islamic fundamentalism could not be studied only as a set of political movements; it must also be viewed as a set of intellectual discourses and critiques of philosophy, political ideology, and science. Its philosophical tradition includes both a belief in the existence of objective and ultimate truth and a claim of limited human subjective understanding of that truth. Furthermore, fundamentalism attempts to offer a way of life and thought based on its understanding of both God's law (sharia) and nature. Its political ideology refutes the notions of both an ultimate human authority and man's possessive nature. Thus, fundamentalism upholds the need for setting up virtuous, just, and equal societies. In this sense, fundamentalists' call for an immediate political project, the Islamic state, are linked to achieving these societies. Whether such a philosophy is well grounded or properly developed, and whether one accepts or rejects fundamentalism, should not make it a passing phenomenon.

One of the commonest prophecies of the mid-1990s (Huntington, 1993:22-49) was that the Muslim world was heading for a fight with other parts of the world that do not share its religio-political opinions: above all, worry nervous Europeans, a fight with Europe. There are good reasons why the culture of the Muslim world is regarded, erroneously, of course, by many people as the West's only real ideological competitor at the end of the 20th century. Islam claims to be an idea based upon a transcendental certainty. The certainty is the word of God, revealed through Angel Gabriel syllable by syllable to Prophet Muhammad in Arabia over 1400 years ago. As a means of binding a civilisation together there is no substitute for such a certainty. Moreover, new recruits are flocking to join this claim to certainty.

Islamic fundamentalism is partly a response to Christo-Western superiority to, and dominance of, the Islamic world, and partly a negation or rejection of folk-religious tradition. Dr Hasan al-Turabi, the leading theoretician of Islamism in North Africa and the Middle

East, argued, for example, that to-date the overall intellectual and historical experience of the Muslims has failed them at all levels; in military confrontations as well as intellectual rigour. This experience has left Muslims incapable of keeping pace with modernity. He further contends that this situation is the outcome of the failure of Muslim thinkers and their intellectual edifices to positively influence development by solving Muslims' problems and meeting their dire needs. In his view, today Muslims live on the fringes of both Islam and western civilisation. Their lives lack both the Islamic religious spirit and the Western technological advancement. 'Lacking in abstract and scientific sciences (Moussalli, 1999:156), Islamic culture and civilisation have long since reached a point of bankruptcy.' To al-Turabi what is needed now is a new and modern Islamic thought that takes into account modernity but simultaneously grounds it in the divine text, not in new or inherited authorities.

Thus (Beedham, 1994:4-5), partly because of the repeated defeats inflicted upon Muslims by the outside world, particularly America and Israel, and, partly because of the modernisation policies of the state, which Islamisists blame for the loss of religious and cultural identity, the past 34 years have seen a huge growth in Islamic fundamentalism. A large number of people who feel ashamed of the past few centuries want to show they can do better. To do that, they need to rediscover a sense of identity. And, to achieve that, they turn back to the Qur'an and the Sunna. You can call it a revival, or a resurgence; but it is also a return to the foundations. This is what has set scalps tingling in other parts of the world, especially among Europeans.

The Islamic fundamentalists (Malik, 2002:2) usually promise a righteous society, here and now, through catharsis: a transformation from corruption to purity, from *jahiliyya* to Islam. Thus, whereas Muslims have traditionally accepted more or less unjust rulers who nominally adhered to Islamic law (Moussalli, 1999:36), the fundamentalists now view revolting against unjust and unelected rulers not only as a political doctrine but also as an ethical obligation.

Revolution (Miller, 1993:43-55) is now loaded with political, ethical, theological, and metaphysical connotations. Its fulfilment becomes a synonym for the righteous application of Islamic teachings. In the view of the fundamentalists, revolution becomes a quest for universal change to bring about justice and happiness, which must not be hindered by any authority.

Revolution is not, however, a synonym for a coup d'etat or a forceful seizure of state power; it is an attempt at a total transformation that changes the way people think and live. Islam regulates all aspects of life and allows for renewed solutions to new problems. It is also a complete system, having social, economic and political laws and regulations. The revolutionary changes that 'true' Islam can bring about are quite many (Peters, 1995): first, it eliminates the persuasive ritualistic paganism, and replaces it with self-sacrifice, love for humanity, and adherence to truth. Second, 'true' Islamic belief leads to honesty and dignity, which prevents Muslims from yielding to tyrannical power, whether of a political or religious nature. Submission to power without proper political, moral, and legal objectives is unacceptable.

Hence, from the fundamentalists' point of view, it is a natural right for people to revolt against evil, and the use of force is justified when obstacles are imposed on this development. In particular, the fundamentalists are concerned with the state's denial of their activities to propagate their understanding of Islam. Freedom to propagate Islam is basic to the fundamentalists who want to call people to their ideas. Any obstruction of propagation of Islam is, thus, equated with standing against Islam itself, since Islam is essentially a call for change towards the divine.

This situation leads to the necessity of setting up a vanguard whose raison d'etre is struggle, or jihad, against the institutions resisting the propagation of Islam. Radical fundamentalists presume that making the truth of Islam known is sufficient to induce people to follow Islamic teachings. Their insistence on people's freedom to adopt any philosophy of life springs from their confidence in Islam's natural appeal. Furthermore, the fundamentalists' insistence on

Islamising every social or political doctrine (Hovsepian, 1995:1-24) is also a quest for identity and for social and political legitimacy. Their rejection of the traditional modes of understanding - such as theology, philosophy, sufism, and jurisprudence (Anawati, 1974: 350-58) - eases the movement toward popular legitimacy which empowers the community to take matters into its own hands and to deligitimise the imposed elites. Most political elites embody a rupture with the past, representing the original interests of colonialist and imperialist powers, and the current interests of world powers. If the Qur'an and the Sunna are the source materials for a comprehensive Islamic revival (Moussalli, 1999:184; and Miller, 1993:43-55), then the removal of these elites is a Qur'anically legitimate matter.

Islamic fundamentalism is actually an umbrella for a wide range of discourses and activism which tend to move from a high level of moderate pluralism, and thus inclusive democracy, to extreme radicalism, intolerant unitarism, and thus exclusive majority rule. While some fundamentalists are politically pluralistic, but theologically exclusive, others are accommodating religiously but direct their exclusivist programme against the outside world - the West or imperialism. More important (Kramer, 1993:2-8; and Lewis, 1993:89-98) while most moderate fundamentalists call for pluralistic democracy and speak in its support as an essentially Islamic point of view, the radicals brand it unbelief.

The inclusive democratic and exclusive authoritarian policies of most Middle Eastern states, along with international powers (Anderson, 1987:1-18), reinforce and, in fact, create this dual nature of fundmentalists' political thought and behaviour. What must distinguish a radical view from a moderate one is the method used to transform a political agenda into daily life. Islamic fundamentalism employs diverse methodological and practical processes to create intellectual and political doctrines. One doctrine is conceptually based on theoretical and practical exclusivity that permits violent means towards the other party. The fact that radical fundamentalism lives in isolation from society in conditions of social disunity, corruption, exploitation, political violence, and undemocratic regimes, it has transformed its political discourse into an isolationist theology of politics. Indeed, fundamentalists, in general, believe that their governments do not serve the ideological, political, or economic interests of their peoples, but instead serve those of the world powers as well as those of national oligarchies.

Liberalisation, whether economic, political, or cultural, as well as social justice, political freedom, and democracy are major demands of both radical and moderate fundamentalist movements. Modern nation-states have been considered by radical fundamentalists as the link between what is unacceptable and inhuman in both Western and Eastern civilisations: Western materialism and Eastern despotism. An Islamic state, they believe, can withstand and even correct Western materialistic domination and Eastern political authoritarianism.

3

Conceptualisation of an Islamic State

The Islamic State and *Shura*

The political system of Islam is unique in its structure, its powers, its functions, and its purpose. It is not pragmatic or instrumentalist. It is not a theocracy, if by theocracy we mean a government or political rule by priests or clergy as representatives of God. Nor is it a proletariat. It is not even a democracy in its popular sense. It is something different from all of these.

The rule of Islam is by no means the rule of theocracy. It is the rule of Islamic law, however vaguely defined. The consensus among Sunni theoreticians of Islamism is against the legitimate existence of an Islamic clergy, who are more than scholars. A proper Islamic rule is no more than the systematic rule of Islamic law where Islamic ideas spread and where Islamic regulations define the forms of government and society. Thus (Moussalli, 1999:43), 'the inherent authority of the clergy is denied by all Sunni fundamentalists'. To describe the proper Islamic government as a theocracy is, therefore, a misnomer, since it gives the wrong impression about Islam. Neither theory nor practice lends credibility to theocracy in Islam. A proper Islamic state is both communal and constitutional: both the judiciary and legislature, as well as the executive entity, rule only through delegated powers by means of shura (consultation).

The Shi'ite brand of Islamic fundamentalism, as advocated by Ayatollah Khomeini, may more appropriately be called theocratic. Khomeini advocates in his *Al-Hukuma al-Islamiyya* (the Islamic government) the legitimate rule of only jurists, because a proper Islamic government must be based on jurisprudence. However, the majority of the fundamentalists rule out the need for a clergy to bestow legitimacy on Islamic government. Its legitimacy springs from adhering to divine governance and from the execution of the sharia. So, while Khomeini views the right to rule as issuing from the Imam (the leader of the whole Muslim community), Sunni fundamentalists view it as delegated authority from the people.

The modern *shura*, as advocated by al-Banna and others, postulates the necessity of people's participation not only in political matters but in all issues concerning the community. Every citizen in an Islamic state is enjoined to offer his best advice on common matters and must be entitled to do so. The seeking of counsel on the part of the ruler, and rendering it on the part of the public, is not a matter of choice or a voluntary measure. It is an article of faith, a religious ordinance. God says (Surah 3:159): '... and consult them in affairs of the moment. Then, when you have taken a decision, put your trust in Allah'. He further says (Surah 5:45): 'And, if any do fail to judge or rule according to what God has revealed, they are the unbelievers - they are the wrongdoers - they are the rebels'. *Shura* denies the legitimacy of authoritarian rule or political monopoly over the Muslim community and makes the community the source of executive power.

Al-Banna argues, for example (see Moussalli, 1999:121), that the ruler, regardless of his social or religious position, must not single-handedly regulate state affairs; in the final analysis, he must resort and yield to people's choices. However, Sayyid Qutb who, until his death in 1966, was the leading theoretician for the Muslim Brotherhood in Egypt, goes a step further by postulating the need for people's participation in public affairs and by demanding the right to elect rulers. He does this through dehistoricising and deconstructing the interpretation of the *shura*. For instance, while Muslim *ulama* (religious scholars) had to nominally approve the ruler's selection, once elected, the ruler had a free hand within the sharia. Moreover, Qutb's argument that *shura* is not specifically defined and that its form is an organisational matter, depending on the needs of every age, has no doctrinal or historical precedent. But under the sultanic concept of authority, on which the existing Islamic states are based, *shura* has been the scholars' domain by advising rulers at the expense of the rest of the Muslim community.

Like Qutb, al-Turabi questions the legitimacy of the historicity of *shura*, arguing that Muslims today are just as capable of producing a theory of the *shura* or consultation, or *ijma'* (consensus) that, though different from previous ones, is, nonetheless, as authentic. For instance, if Muslims were now to use consultation, as practised historically, they would not be served well, since historically it meant the consultation of the elites, whereas today's use of consultation must imply a universal process. In al-Turabi's opinion (see Moussalli, 1999:161), 'restricting consultation to scholars only, as was the case in the recent past, is suited neither to modernity nor to the ambitions of the people'.

For the radicals, the *shura* not only becomes a religious doctrine or a mechanism for elections, but also reflects public will, a doctrine much superior to individual freedom or social agreement. More importantly, it represents the divine will, and any deviation from the divine is a religious violation. The individual cannot but submit to this will; in fact, he is only an appendage to it, with his freedom dependent on it. While this 'will' may opt for a political contract with a ruler, it cannot, because of what it represents, allow pluralism and basic differences leading to disunity. The establishment of an Islamic state becomes, for radicalism, the fulfilment of this divine will, and individuals and groups are, consequently, subordinated to the state. Judged through the lens of the sharia, the institutionalisation of *shura* and *ijma'* provides the state, which expresses the general will of the people, with a normative role in making basic choices in people's lives. The formal legitimacy that the state acquires makes it, in fact, unaccountable to anybody but God or obedience to the sharia, itself institutionalised in the state. The purpose of *shura* is, therefore, to ensure that the sharia is observed, and that the rights of citizens are honoured and their obligations fulfilled.

Islam and Politics

The political system of Islam is based on two cardinal principles. Firstly, every deed of Muslims individually and collectively must be inspired and guided by the Qur'an, which is the constitution chosen by God for His true servants, i.e. the Muslims. Thus the Qur'an is the constitution of the Islamic state, and Muslims are ordained by God to handle their common affairs through the *shura* (consultation).

The perfection of a Muslim's creed must lead him to act on behalf of society. And, Islam's comprehensiveness makes it fit for human *fitra* (innate disposition) and capable of influencing, not only the masses, but also the elites. Islam provides the most worldly and just principles, and the straightest of divine legal codes and, as such, it uplifts the human soul and sanctifies universal brotherhood. Islam also offers practical ways to achieve all this in people's daily lives, social living, education and political aspirations. It is on this basis that Islam bases its state and establishes its universal call to humankind. While Islam asks humans to satisfy themselves spiritually and materially, it provides them with regulations that prevent extreme behaviour to help the believer arrive at a balanced fulfilment. Thus, diverse Islamic regulations satisfy different needs: the economic regulations, for material well-being; the political, for unity, justice, and freedom, and also for social equality. These regulations are only fractions of the authentic Islamic method.

What distinguishes Islam from most other religions is its concern with not only worship but also the social system. To al-Banna (see Moussalli, 1999:08), 'Islam is thus comprised of creed, worship, and governance and is a collective and state religion'. Islam as a social system deals with all social phenomena and, as such, the Qur'an and the Sunna must represent the highest fundamental authority and point of reference. Islam is concerned with all aspects of life and postulates precise methods, fundamentals, and foundations for humankind. It is simply a general code for all races, peoples, and nations. Islam provides, first, the hope needed in the building of nations; second, the national pride needed to create a good image of the self; and third, the power needed for defence.

From al-Banna's point of view, activism is the sign of good belief and political action should be in line with Islamic teachings. In fact, separating Islam from politics is not Islamic. Theoretically, Islam is more comprehensive than politics and absorbs it. Individual perfection requires politicising Islam. In this sense, Islam is a complete, active religion that must relate to all aspects of life. From al-Banna's perspective (see Moussalli, 1999: 109), Islam must act as a regulator of behaviour of both Muslim communities and all human societies. Its general goals are designed to fit all societies, and this can be done through reinterpretation of texts to suit different times and ages. Islam aims, then, at setting up a good nation with a message of unity and sacrifice. There is no religiously real nation today, since territory, race, language, and material interests are not adequate. One of the most important aspects of Islam is its capability to unite humankind on a religious basis and to do away with racial, linguistic, territorial and cultural differences. Thus religion should be the Muslims' nationality.

The link between religion and politics is supported by Qur'anic verses, among which are the following: *Surah* 4: 105, *Surah* 5: 44-45, 47, 48, and 50, and *Surah* 24: 51. These scriptural references constitute the legitimacy of Islamic rule and its functions: promoting the spiritual, political, and economic well-being, as well as defence of the community. The Qur'an says (Surah 4: 105) for example:

> We have sent down
> To thee the Book in truth,
> That thou mightest judge
> Between people by that which
> Allah has shown thee; so be not
> An advocate for those
> Who betray their trust.

Furthermore, its function is extended worldwide and, therefore, the state universalises the Islamic call. Consequently, the well-being of humankind as a concern of the Islamic call, makes the role of the Islamic state both moral and universal.

An Islamic state is the essential first step for achieving the good Islamic society. Without the state, society would find many difficulties in voluntarily organising itself on an Islamic basis, since the nature of many basic Islamic doctrines requires an organising agency of the first rate. Within modern geographical realities, that agency is the Islamic state. It is only the state that can function as both an executive agency that remedies all problems and as an institution that develops Islamic laws suitable for this age. Indeed, the perception of Islam as 'a complete system regulating all aspects of life including a system of social norms, government, legislation, and education'. cannot be realised without the state. It is equally true that mere religiosity without a solid commitment to political, social, and economic activism is useless to the community of Muslims.

In fact, in al-Banna's opinion (see (Moussalli, 1999, 119), the absence of a commitment to political Islam is *jahiliyya*. He subordinates the legitimacy of the state to the fulfilment of the basic Islamic goals which, among other things, include a commitment to apply Islamic law and the spread of the Islamic call, thus linking religious commitment to political legitimacy. Therefore, the legitimacy of any political authority stems from political rule in accordance with the Qur'an and the principles of Islamic jurisprudence.

Thus, the call to Islam is a moral and religious duty that must be carried out privately by the community and officially by the Islamic government. But it is the government that must carry out the broader essentials of the 'Islamic Call' - that is, addressing the general moral or spiritual atmosphere within the *ummah* (community) and curbing moral and political degeneration and atheistic orientations. In this sense, the government becomes the executive arm of the virtuous society, and, by trust, it enacts the society's moral, religious, and political objectives. By following the demands of a virtuous society, the state does not produce conflicting claims but becomes the popular, guiding, social, executive power in charge of executing just laws. Only by playing such a role can the necessary conditions for the legitimacy of government be fulfilled. By contrast, in Western civilisation, the state is an institutionalised structure of domination and coordination of both law-and-order and development types of activities.

The purpose of the Islamic state, therefore, is to administer justice and to provide security and protection for all citizens, regardless of colour or race or creed, in conformity with the stipulations of the Qur'an. Consequently, the Islamic state cannot be controlled by a political party of a non-Islamic platform or be subjected to foreign powers. It is incompatible with Islam, therefore, for a Muslim nation to pledge support to any political party of a non-Islamic platform or to yield to a non-Islamic government of alien-originated aims. The Qur'an makes it clear (Surah 42:39) that believers are those who, when an oppressive wrong is inflicted on them, are not cowed, but defend themselves until victory.

But Muslims and Islamic states are also encouraged to co-operate with non-Muslims and non-Muslim states, particularly those that have given asylum to Muslims. If a Muslim community suffers voluntary exile on account of persecution and oppression, for example, and some of its weaker members stay behind, holding fast to faith but not prepared for the higher sacrifice, the exiles still have a duty to help their weaker brethren in matters of religion. The exiles, being at open war against the state which oppressed them, would be free to fight against such a state. But (commentary no 1241) if the weaker brethren are in a state in mutual alliance with the Muslim community, the community cannot in honour interfere with that state, whether it is Muslim or not. In fact, the Qur'an states (Surah 8:72) that Muslim exiles have a duty to help fellow Muslims who did not migrate except against a people with whom the Muslim community has a treaty of mutual alliance. Consultative methods in politics are not only a democratic formula of government, but a religious injunction and a moral duty enjoined upon the rulers as well as the ruled.

Under the political system of Islam every citizen is entitled to enjoy freedom of belief and conscience, and freedom of thought and expression. He is free to develop his potentialities and improve his lot, to work and compete, to earn and possess property, to approve and disapprove of things, according to his honest judgement. But his freedom is not, and cannot be absolute; or else it amounts to chaos and anarchy. It is guaranteed and governed by the sharia. As long as it is in line with this law, it is the rightful privilege of every individual citizen; but if it transgresses the limits of the law or conflicts with the common interest, it becomes a violation of the sharia and must, therefore, be controlled.

Thus, though the individual pursuit of things is legitimate, yet freedom must not mean animalistic and individualistic actions in order to attain particular earthly gains. In fact, this poses a danger to the society and constitutes the very opposite of freedom, enslaving humans to their lower instincts and obscuring their vision of true freedom.

An individual whose main goal in life is pleasure cannot claim to be free. For freedom comes only from liberty, whose essence is the individual's foregoing animalistic pleasure and living the life of *tawhid* (oneness of God). Freedom should be rooted in, and justified by, the divine text.

In Islam, freedom, as well as what it entails, is both metaphysical and doctrinal; that is, freedom is a religious doctrine whose violation goes beyond mere political violation to constitute a violation of something divine. In liberalism, however, freedom is a legal and political concept but never a religious or divine one. Thus, Islamic discourse does not speak only of the interests of individuals or their fears of government. It also speaks of popular consciousness, whose strengthening serves as a guarantee against any violation of political rule that bestows on itself communal powers. In this sense, *shura* becomes a liberating religious doctrine which cannot be claimed by political authority and which must rule only contractually and in the service of the social order.

Secondly, the sovereignty in the Islamic state does not belong to the ruler nor even to the people themselves. It belongs to God, and the people as a whole exercise it by trust from Him to enforce His law and enact His Will. The ruler is not a sovereign over the people. He is a viceroy chosen by the people. He derives his authority from his obedience to the sharia, which binds the rulers and the ruled alike by a solemn contract over which God is the supervisor. Islamic universalism is underpinned by the doctrine of God's *hakimiyya* (divine governance) which postulates the absolute sovereignty of God over the universe. Thus no legitimate lawgiver exists but Him. He alone has the right to command or forbid.

The rulers who are chosen by the people to administer the sharia are entitled to support and obedience from the people but only if they observe the sharia. If the administration swerves from the path of God, or fails to observe the sharia, it is not only committing an offence against God, but also has no right to the support and loyalty of the public. And, whereas the formal aspect of the government's function is to regulate human affairs in accordance with the sharia and the individual is obliged to obey the government, obedience cannot be unconditional or absolute. Non-adherence to Islamic law by the government, for example (Moussalli, 1949: 141), removes any formal legitimacy and creates sufficient grounds for disobedience and revolution by the ruled, i.e. Muslims.

For instance, when a Muslim community is ruled by laws other than its own, a clash is bound to erupt between it and the ruling party, thus posing difficulties for believers in accepting a secular ruler. Professor Adamu (Adamu, 2001:2) has aptly observed, for instance, that 'the act of entrenching secularism in a Muslim community is also an act of de-Islamising the members of that community; for in a society in which secularism reigns supreme, such as the Ugandan society …, Islam cannot be successfully practised as a complete way of life that it really is.' Obedience to those charged with authority is, therefore, conditional on their own obedience to the sharia and the *Sunna*. In one of his conclusive statements, Prophet Muhammad said that 'there could be no obedience or loyalty to any human being, ruler or otherwise, who is not himself obedient to God and bound by His law.' Thus, if the government betrays the trust of God and the public, it has no right to continue in office. It must be ousted from power and replaced by an Islamic government. And, it is the responsibility of every Muslim citizen to see to it that this is done in the public interest.

The rulers and administrators must be chosen from among the best qualified citizens on the basis of their own merits of virtue, fitness and competence. The candidates may be chosen by public consent through general elections, or they may be selected and authorised by public leaders, who are, in turn, entrusted with leadership by the free accord of the various sections of society. Thus, an Islamic state can have as many representative councils or municipal administrators as may be deemed necessary.

And, although the ruler is chosen and appointed by the people, his first responsibility is to God and, then, to the people. However, his office is not just symbolic nor is his role simply ceremonial. He is not a helpless puppet to execute the public will, whether it is right or wrong. He must exercise real state powers on behalf of the people for their best interest in accordance with the law of God. He has a dual responsibility. On one hand, he is accountable to God for his conduct, and on the other, he is responsible to the people who have put their trust in him. Indeed in Islam, the state headship is first and foremost an obligation, a trying commitment, an awesome responsibility.

But, both the ruler and his people will also have to give full account before God as to how they treated the Qur'an and how they treated the law of God which He has given to mankind as a binding force. The ruler is not to govern the people according to their own desires. He is to serve them by making justice a common law and by making their genuine obedience to the sovereign Lord of the universe a regular function of the state, and by making sound morality a noble undertaking of the government.

The governorship of the Islamic state is a public trust, with which the administrators are entrusted by the word of God as well as the common consent of the people. With God being the supreme sovereign of the state, whoever represents Him in the top office, must be a believer, i.e. a Muslim. And, with the majority of the people being Muslims, whoever assumes the office of president must be a true Muslim. These measures are taken to serve the common interest and to fulfil all obligations of the state to God as well as to the people. They are also taken to secure and honour the rights of the religious or racial minorities. Hence, the political system of Islam is fundamentally different from all other political systems and doctrines known to mankind.

4

Religio-political Rights of Muslims under an Islamic State

An Introductory Comment

In Chapter 3 an attempt was made to define the powers of an Islamic state and its responsibilities and functions. Also, some attention was given to identifying the type of leadership that is necessary for the success of an Islamic state in wielding its powers and in performing its functions under the sovereignty of Allah. In addition, it was observed that the citizenry of an Islamic state, most of whom would be Muslim, have duties to their fellow men, to the state, and finally to Allah. Of course, every upright Muslim is required and expected to perform his duties conscientiously, whether to his fellow men or to the state or to Allah. This is because in each case he is performing a form of worship, a religious duty ordained by Allah. And while under an Islamic state Muslims are facilitated as a matter of course and, of course, might even be compelled by the state to perform their duties, the situation under a non-Islamic state, as is the case in Uganda, is bound to be less favourable for Muslims to practise their faith freely without any hindrance from the state. The religio-political and social rights of Muslims, which under an Islamic state are taken for granted, may only be secured under non-Islamic regimes by pertinacious and forceful support for these rights by a systemised Muslim population. But, it is also possible to achieve these rights through negotiations with a non-Islamic government, especially if it is a just one.

But, for a Muslim population to successfully protect its rights against encroachment by a non-Islamic state, it must be very knowledgeable about these rights or else it will easily lose the argument to its detractors. Fair enough, less informed proponents of a course of action are usually more impetuous than well-informed ones. The past three decades have witnessed a growing interest in the rights of Muslims in Uganda and, simultaneously, an increased focus on the practices of Islam. This Islamic awakening, as shown in Chapter 6, is part and parcel of a worldwide Islamic Resurgence which is an effort to find solutions to societal problems not in Western ideologies but in Islam. This book provides a collation of the religio-political rights of Muslims in an ideal environment with research results on the practice of these rights in Uganda. The book's analysis of the rights of Muslims makes it a useful resource for readers interested in the advancement of Islam in East Africa in general and in Uganda in particular.

And, although Islam is truly 'a way of life' for those who believe in it, since a Muslim's entire life is guided by Qur'anic injunctions, the present discussion is not intended to give a comprehensive analysis of the duties and rights of the Muslims. Rather, the aim of this chapter is to provide a survey of those rights which either infringe on national laws or promote conflicts between Muslims and non-Muslims, particularly Christians, here in Uganda. In the context of the present discussion (Gove et al. eds, 1986:1955) the term 'right' refers to something to which one has a just claim or something that justly accrues or falls to one, such as:

1. The power or privilege to which one is just entitled (as upon principles of morality, religion, law, or custom).

2. A power, privilege, or condition of existence to which one has a natural claim of enjoyment or possession (the rights of the people).

3. A power, privilege, or immunity vested in one (as by authority or social custom).

4. A power or privilege vested in a person by the law to demand action or forebearance at the hands of another: a capacity or privilege the enjoyment of which is secured to a person by law.

The religio-political rights discussed in this study fall in one of these classifications.

The Right to be Ruled by a Fellow Muslim

Considering that the aim of an Islamic state is to administer justice and to provide security and protection for all citizens ... in conformity with the stipulation of God in His constitution, the Qur'an;

Considering also that besides its perceived role as the all-round provider, government is also seen as the custodian of values, and the supreme defender of the faith;

Considering also that the ruler is not a sovereign over the people and that he is only an acting executive chosen by people to serve them according to the sharia, and that he derives his authority from his obedience to the sharia;

Considering further that rulers are to be obeyed and helped by the public as long as they themselves obey God, and that they have no claims to obedience from the people if they were to depart from the way of God;

Considering finally that God supports (Surah 22:41):

> (They are) those who,
> If We establish them
> in the land, establish
> Regular prayer and give
> Zakat, enjoin
> The right and forbid wrong:
> With Allah rests the end
> (And decision) of (all) affairs.

It is obvious that the governorship of an Islamic state is a public trust with which the administrators are entrusted by the word of God as well as by the common consent of the people so that whoever assumes the office of president must be a 'true Muslim.' It is incompatible with Islam, therefore, for a Muslim nation or community to pledge support to any political party of a non-Islamic platform or to yield to a non-Islamic government of alien aims.

In political terms, piety entails, as the Qur'an suggests, showing compassion and love to all people. A pious ruler makes compassion the pillar of his government, and a fundamental principle in human relations. We are told, for instance, that (Sulaiman, 1988:3) 'You will see no one, under the government of a pious leader, driven to destitution or banished into the streets as a beggar, without honour. People's lives are not ruined nor their meagre possessions wiped out by cruel economic policies'. In this regard, Islam demands that rulers should regard their responsibilities as an act of worship, not a means for self-aggrandisement.

And, with God being the Supreme Sovereign of the state, whoever represents Him in the top office must be faithful, i.e. a Muslim. Herein lies the Muslims' right to be ruled by a fellow Muslim. In Islam, the state headship is first and foremost an obligation, a trying commitment, an awesome responsibility. It would be inequitable, therefore, if Islam were to impose such responsibilities upon non-Muslims.

The Right to be Ruled in Accordance with the Sharia

Considering that every deed of the Muslim individual or group of individuals must be inspired and guided by the sharia and the Qur'an which is the constitution chosen by God for His true servants;

Considering further that both the ruler and his people will also have to give full account before God of how they treated the Qur'an and the sharia;

Considering also that the seeking of counsel on the part of the ruler and rendering it on the part of the public is not a matter of choice or a voluntary measure, but an article of Faith, a religious ordinance;

Considering too that the sovereignty in the Islamic state belongs to God, and the people as a whole exercise it by trust from Him to enforce the sharia and enact His Will;

It is imperative that Muslims, who by definition are those who submit to Allah alone, and pledge loyalty, administer the sharia and observe its stipulation, should be ruled in accordance with the sharia and not under any other political system. Otherwise they will fail in their duty as Muslims with the responsibility to hearken to their Lord, and establish regular payer, and conduct their affairs by mutual consultation. It is out of this obligation that Muslims derive the right to be governed in accordance with the sharia.

The Right to Say the Five Canonical Prayers and to Attend the Jumu'a Prayer

Prayer stands as the pillar of the faith that is next to the profession of faith in importance. There are two kinds of prayer: the spontaneous, extemporaneous one prompted by the exigencies of the situation, and the five canonical prayers. These are formal, institutional ones for which ceremonial cleanliness, involving ablution, is a prerequisite. The five canonical prayers are legally prescribed at stated times and performed with specified bodily gestures and genuflections and with orientation towards Mecca. These prayers are synchronised with the muezzin's call to prayer five times a day. Its object is not so much petitioning God for favours, as it is glorifying Him and acknowledging His oneness, His might and majesty. The bodily movements culminate in prostrating oneself to the point of touching the ground with the forehead. Mosque is a corruption of *masjid*, meaning place of prostration. The number five (at dawn, noon, mid-afternoon, sunset, and early evening) for the daily obligation prayers was arrived at on the occasion of Muhammad's miraculous ascent to heaven. The Qur'an says (Surah 62:9):

> When the call is proclaimed
> To prayer on Friday
> (The Day of Assembly)
> Hasten earnestly to the Remembrance
> Of Allah, and leave off
> Business (and traffic):
> That is best for you
> If ye but knew!

The Qur'an further says (Surah 62:10):

> And when the Prayer
> Is finished, then may ye
> Disperse through the land,
> And seek of the Bounty
> Of Allah: and
> Remember Allah frequently
> That ye may prosper.

And, as Yusuf Ali tells us, Friday is, primarily, the weekly meeting of the congregation, when Muslims show their unity by sharing in common public worship, preceded by a *khutba*, in which the Imam (a prayer-leader) reviews the week's life of the community and offers advice and exhortation on good living that is rich in Qur'anic quotations. The idea behind the Muslim weekly day of assembly is different from that behind the Jewish Sabbath (Saturday) or the Christian Sunday.

The Jewish Sabbath is primarily a commemoration of God's ending His work and resting on the seventh day. However, Islam teaches that Allah needs no rest, nor does He feel fatigue. In part the Qur'an says (Surah 2: 255): '... His Throne doth extend over the heavens and the earth, and He feeleth no fatigue in guarding and preserving them ....' The Islamic faith, on the other hand, lays chief emphasis on the remembrance of Allah during the *Jumu'a* prayer. And, although the Christian Church has changed the day from Saturday to Sunday, nevertheless, it inherited the Jewish spirit. The Islamic teaching tells Muslims (Islamic Researches, 1992: commentary no. 5462) that, when the time for the *Jumu'a* prayer comes, they should close their business and answer the summon loyally and earnestly, meet earnestly, pray, consult and learn by social contact; and that, when the meeting is over, they should scatter and go about their business. This notwithstanding, Friday is a public holiday in many Islamic countries in the Middle East, including Saudi Arabia. But here the main motive is convenience rather than the necessity to fulfil a religious duty.

So, only one weekly *Jumu'a* prayer is enjoined, i.e. the one on Friday at noon. Women's attendance (Hitti, 1970:34) is not obligatory. The worshippers are required to stand in rows, with spaces in between for prostration, and to chant the ritual in union.

The Muslims are equally obliged to say the five canonical prayers daily during specified periods. The morning prayer is the *Fajr*. It is said after the light is up but before sunrise (6.00 a.m.). The early afternoon prayer, *Zuhr*, is said immediately after noon (1.00 p.m.). The late afternoon prayer, *Asr*, is said about 4.00 p.m. The evening prayer, *Magrib*, is said just after sunset (7.00 p.m.). The early night prayer, *Isha*, is said at suppertime when the glow of sunset is disappearing (8.00 p.m.). These are the five canonical prayers of Islam. The times change from season to season and from place to place, however. The times given here are applicable to Uganda. The five canonical prayers are obligatory for all Muslims. The Qur'an says (Surah 11:114):

> And establish regular prayers
> At the two ends of the day
> And at the approaches of the night:
> For those things that are good
> Remove those that are evil:
> That is a reminder
> For the mindful.

Considering that Islam teaches that man is merely a trustee in the vast domain of God, and that the sole purpose of his creation is to worship God;

Considering also that Muslims truly believe that the Arabic copy of the Qur'an that a Muslim uses today is an exact replica of a heavenly prototype dictated word by word to the Prophet Muhammad;

It is crystal clear that Surah 62 verses 9 and 10 and Surah 11: 114 quoted above, impose an obligation upon Muslims to attend the *Jumu'a* prayer on Friday at noon and to say the daily five canonical prayers. From this obligation, then, arises the right for one's attendance at the *Jumu'a* prayer, and to say the five canonical prayers of Islam daily since failure to do so would be a serious breach of Quar'anic injunctions.

The Right to Fast during the Ramadhan

Ramadhan, the ninth month of the Islamic calender, was fixed as a month of fasting. The Qur'an says (Surah 2:185):

> Ramadhan is the (month)
> in which was sent down
> The Qur'an, as a guide
> To mankind, also clear (signs)
> For guidance and judgement
> (Between right and wrong).
> So every one of you
> Who is present (at his home)
> During that month
> Should spend it in fasting,
> But if anyone is ill,
> Or on a journey,
> The prescribed period
> (Should be made up)
> By days later.
> Allah intends every facility
> For you; He does not want
> To put you to difficulties,
> (He wants you) to complete
> The prescribed period,
> And to glorify Him
> In that He has guided you;
> And perchance ye shall be grateful.

Ramadhan is the ninth month of the Muslim lunar year and progressively moves through all seasons of the solar year. Since food and drink (as well as sexual relations) are forbidden from the time a white thread can be distinguished from a black thread till sunset, fasting becomes particularly trying when it occurs in summer. The beginning of the month is marked by the appearance of the new moon. Customarily sunrise and sunset are proclaimed in Uganda by a muezzin who uses the human voice with or without the aid of an electric loudspeaker to call Muslims to prayer.

Abstinence, primarily an act of self-denial, when used for expiation commands a high value. A *hadith* (the authentic sayings of Prophet Muhammad) in al-Bukhari promises forgiveness of all past sins to him who keeps Ramadhan in faith and for Allah's sake. Undoubtedly, *Surah* 2 verse 185 quoted above, imposes an obligation upon Muslims, with the exception of those who are sick or on a journey, to fast during Ramadhan. Since failure to do so would be in breach of a Qur'anic injunction, the obligation to fast during Ramadhan, to which Muslims are justly entitled, becomes their right. The end of fasting, which is marked as the Id al-Fitr, is celebrated throughout the Muslim world, including Uganda where it is an official public holiday.

The Right to Go on the Hajj

The Hajj is another institution which lends itself to public display, and it is the fifth pillar of the Islamic faith. Hence those Muslims who have the ability to do so are required to perform the Hajj to the holy city of Mecca. The Qur'an says (Surah 2:196):

> And complete
> The Hajj or umra
> In the service of Allah,
> But if ye are prevented
> (From completing it),
> Send an offering
> For sacrifice,
> Such as ye may find,
> And do not shave your heads
> Until the offering reaches
> The place of sacrifice.
> And if any of you is ill,
> Or has an ailment in his scalp
> (Necessitating shaving),
> (He should) in compensation

Either fast, or feed the poor,
Or offer sacrifice;
And when ye are
In peaceful condition (again),
If any one wishes
To continue the umra
On to the Hajj,
He must make an offering
Such as he can afford,
But if he cannot afford it,
He should fast
Three days during the Hajj
And seven days on his return.
This is for those
Whose household
Is not in (the precincts)
Of the sacred Mosque.
And fear Allah.
And know that Allah,
Is strict in punishment.

The hajj is the complete pilgrimage, of which the chief rites are performed during the first thirteen days of the month of *Zul-hajjah*, the twelfth month of the lunar year to which the pilgrimage gives its name. The *umrah* is a less formal pilgrimage which can be performed at any time of the year. In either case, the intending pilgrim commences by putting on a simple garment of unsewn white cloth in two pieces when he is some distance away from Mecca. The putting on of this pilgrim garb (*ihram*) symbolises the pilgrim's renunciation of the vanities of the world. After this and until the end of the Hajj, he must not wear other clothes, or ornaments, anoint his hair, use perfumes, hunt, or do other prohibited acts.

The months of *Shawwal, Zul-qada,* and *Zul-hijjah* up to the 10th or 13th day are set aside for the rites of the Hajj. The first rites may begin as early as the beginning of *Shawwal*, with a definite approach to Mecca. But the chief rites take place during the first ten days of *Zul-hijjah*, especially on the 8th, 9th and 10th days of that month, when the concourse of pilgrims reaches its climax. The main rites of the Hajj (Islamic Researches, 1992: commentary no. 217) include the wearing of the *ihram* from certain points specified on all the roads leading to Mecca, after which the pilgrimage prohibitions come into force and the pilgrim is dedicated to worship and prayer and the denial of vanities; the going round the Ka`ba seven times typifying activity, with the kissing of the little 'Black Stone' built into the wall, the symbol of concentration in the love of Allah; the great Sermon (*Khutba*) on the 7th day of *Zul-hijjah*, when the whole assembly listens to an exposition of the meaning of the Hajj; and the tenth day of *Zul-hijjah*, the Id-ul-Adhha, the day of sacrifice, when the sacrifice of a sheep or other horned domestic animal is offered in the valley of Mina, the head is shaved or the hair trimmed. The completion of the hajj is marked by the shaving of the head for men and the cutting off of a few locks of the hair of the head for women, the taking off of the *ihram* and the resumption of the ordinary dress.

Once a pilgrim undertakes the pilgrimage (Islamic Researches, 1992: commentaries nos. 212 and 213) he must complete it, and he must do it not for worldly ends, but as a symbol of his service of and worship of Allah. But if he is prevented for any reason from completing the rites, a sacrifice should be offered where the prevention took place. And if anyone is taken ill after putting on the *ihram*, so that he has to put on other clothes, or if he has trouble or skin disease in his head or insects in his hair, and he has to shave his head before the completion of the Hajj, he should fast (three days) or feed the poor, or offer sacrifice.

Once a year at the proper time, Mecca becomes so religiously magnetised that it attracts millions of men and women from the four quarters of the globe. From north and south, east and west, they converge on the city by caravan, airplane, or ship. At present (2005) the total number of participants in the annual pilgrimage is over two million people, of whom half come from outside the Arabian peninsula. The social, economic, and intellectual effects of such gatherings are not easy to exaggerate. As believers – black and white, Arabs, Turks, Persians, rich and poor, high and low –worship together, they heighten their awareness of the solidarity of Islam as a religious fraternity. Once at least in a lifetime, where possible, a Muslim shares in the vast international assemblage of the world, in the centre of Islam, during the Meccan pilgrimage.

It is quite clear from *Surah* 2 verse 196 quoted above, that Muslims, both men and women, who are physically fit and have the financial means, are under a religious obligation to answer the Qur'anic call to 'complete the Hajj' to the holy city of Mecca at least once in a lifetime. This is because failure to do so, for whatever reason, other than those sanctioned by the Quar'an, i.e. illness or lack of material means, or both, would be in breach of Qur'anic injunctions which a true Muslim could not take lightly. Herein lies the right of Muslims to perform the Hajj to the holy city of Mecca.

The Right to Wage a Jihad of the Sword

The jihad of the sword, i.e. war, aims at enforcing correct observances of Islamic principles and ritual practices as well as enforcing the sharia. The jihad of the sword can be waged against Muslims accused of half-heartedness or apostasy. The consensus among radical Muslim jurists (see, e.g., Hasan al-Turabi, 1999) is that Muslim rulers who obstruct the way of Islam and put worldly standards before Islam, are rebels against whom the jihad of the sword is legitimate. The jihad of the sword is a duty on the upright and conscientious Muslims. The Qur'an says (Surah 8:38.):

> Say to the Unbelievers,
> If (now) they desist (from unbelief),
> Their past would be forgiven them;
> But if they persist, the punishment
> Of those before them is already
> (A matter of warning for them).

The Qur'an also says (Surah 2:193):

> And fight them on
> Until there is no more Persecution,

> And the religion becomes Allah's.
> But if they cease,
> Let there be no hostility
> Except to those
> Who practise oppression.

The Qur'an further says ((Surah 9:29):

> Fight those who believe not
> In Allah nor the Last Day,
> Nor hold that forbidden
> Which hath been forbidden
> By Allah and His Messenger,
> Nor acknowledge the Religion
> Of Truth, from among
> The People of the Book [i.e. the Bible],
> Until they pay the jizya
> With willing submission,
> And feel themselves subdued.

War is permissible in self-defence, and within well-defined limits. When undertaken, it must be pursued with vigour, but not relentlessly, and only to restore peace and freedom for the worship of Allah. In any case, strict limits must not be transgressed: women, children, the old and infirm men should not be molested, nor trees and crops cut down, nor peace withheld when the enemy comes to terms. If the opposite party ceases to persecute Muslims, they in turn must end hostility with them as a party, but it does not mean that they become friends of oppressors. The armed jihad is against wrong: there should be no rancour against men. Generally speaking, it may be said that Islam (see Islamic Researches, 1992: commentaries nos. 204 and 205) is the religion of peace, goodwill, mutual understanding, and good faith. But it will not acquiesce in wrong-doing, and its men will hold their lives cheap in defence of honour, justice, and the religion which they hold sacred. They believe in courage, obedience, discipline, duty, and a constant striving by all the means in their power – physical, moral, intellectual, and spiritual – for the establishment of truth and righteousness.

Considering that there is no obedience or loyalty to any human being, ruler or otherwise, who is not himself obedient to God and bound by the sharia; and

Considering also that the Qur'an (Surah 42:36-39) urges Muslims who are oppressed not to be cowed but rather to defend themselves until victory;

It is a truism that, if the government betrays the trust of God and the public, it has no right to continue in office. It must be ousted from power and replaced by another government that is more committed to adhering to Islamic principles and practices. And, it is the responsibility of every citizen to see to it that this is done in the public interest.

Indeed the duty to wage a jihad of the sword against legitimate targets is imposed on Muslims in their individual capacities and not on the state per se. There is a well-known divine promise:

> Jihad is your bounden duty; for there is naught like it, and, as for the like of him who wages war in the path of God ... God is most knowing to who fights in his path ... just as he is about him who makes the right prayer in the fast, God has guaranteed to the jihadists (*mujahidun*) in His path that He will give him the Garden where enduring pleasure will be his ... or else He will bring him home safe with reward of booty. There will be no possibility of loss for those who wage jihad.

The jihad may require fighting in God's name, as a form of self-sacrifice. But its essence consists in:

1. A true and sincere Faith, which so fixes its gaze on God, that all selfish or wordly motives seem paltry and fade away.

2. An earnest and ceaseless activity, involving the sacrifice (if need be) of life, person, or property, in the service of God.

Mere brutal fighting is opposed to the whole spirit of the jihad. Thus, while the jihad aims at transforming any institution that does not allow Islam to be freely practised, it is neither suicidal nor a campaign of atrocities. It should be very carefully prepared and fought for very clear 'defence aims' that promote the establishment of the Islamic order wherever possible. Hence, where it is likely to succeed, the jihad of the sword is a duty for upright Muslims. In fact, the Muslim community is forbidden by the sharia to live under the rule of a non-Muslim ruler, whether Christian or Jew, except under the concept of pretended acquiescence (*taqiyya*). The Quar'an says (Surah 60:13):

> O ye who believe!
> Turn not (for friendship)
> To people on whom
> Is the Wrath of Allah.
> Of the Hereafter they are
> Already in despair, just as
> The Unbelievers are
> In despair about those
> (Buried) in graves.

It is, therefore, obligatory for Muslims to withdraw from the land of unbelievers (*dar-al-harb*) or to wage the jihad of the sword against them. The Prophet Muhammad said: 'He who associates with the heathens or lives with them, is just like them', by reference implying that waging the armed jihad of the sword against legitimate targets is the Muslims' obligation to their Lord. Thus, from the Muslims' point of view, migration from the land of persecution is an act of resistance!

Surah 60, from which the above verse is quoted, deals specifically with the kind of social relations which should exist between the Muslim community and unbelievers. The date of the revelation of this *Surah* was about A.H.8, soon after the pagan autocracy of Mecca had treacherously broken the peace treaty of Hudaibiya, which they had made with the Muslim community in the month of *Zul-qa'da* A.H.6. The treaty stipulated, among other things (for the terms of this treaty see the introduction to Surah 48), that the Prophet and his party were not to enter Mecca that year, but that they could enter the City unarmed the following year (A.H.7) to perform the lesser Hajj. And, although in A.H.7 the Prophet and his party were allowed to enter Mecca to perform the lesser pilgrimage, nevertheless, the pagan autocracy of Mecca broke the peace treaty by attacking the Banu Khuza'a tribe which was allied to the Prophet. This led to the conquest of Mecca and the subsequent demise of the Meccan pagan autocracy.

The essence of *Surah* 60, and verse 13 in particular, is that a distinction should be made between those who persecute Muslims because of their faith and want to destroy them and their faith, and those who have shown no such rancour. The enemies of Islam, who would exterminate Muslims and their faith, are not fit objects of Muslims' love, but with those unbelievers who show no rancour, Muslims should deal with them with kindness and justice. And, even though Muslims are expected to treat those unbelievers who have no ill-will towards Muslims and their faith with kindness and justice, they are also expected to withdraw from the land of persecutors and oppressors of Muslims and to wage an armed jihad against them in self-defence or self-preservation.

However, whether or not Muslims could declare a jihad of the sword on unbelievers would depend on the latter's persistence in unbelief or their failure to pay *jizya*. *Jizya* is a tribute or poll-tax (see Islamic Researches, 1992: commentary no 1281) levied on those who do not accept Islam, but are otherwise willing to live under the protection of an Islamic authority (as *dhimmis*) and thus are tacitly willing to submit to its ideals being enforced in the Islamic state. There is no amount permanently fixed for it. *Jizya* is an acknowledgement that those whose religion is tolerated would in their turn not interfere with the preaching and progress of Islam. Being a tax on able-bodied males of military age, *jizya* was in a sense a commutation for military service. So, if unbelievers pay *jizya* or 'desist from unbelief', their past would be forgiven them and they would be spared the atrocious effects of the jihad.

And, in the light of what has been said so far, it is quite clear that Muslims have a just claim, i.e. a right, to wage and participate in a jihad against legitimate targets, for example oppressors and persecutors of Muslims, and those who wage wars of aggression against Muslims, and supporters of Satan, in self-defence or self-preservation. But, when war becomes necessary, Muslims are commanded to exercise self-restraint as much as possible. It is realised that force is a dangerous weapon. Hence, while force may have to be used for self-defence or self-preservation, Muslims must always remember that self-restraint 'is pleasing in the eyes of God.' Moreover, when Muslims fight, it should be for a principle, not out of passion.

The Right to Pay *Zakat*

The Holy Qur'an says (Surah 2:277), for example:

> Those who believe,
> And do deeds of righteousness,
> And establish regular prayers
> And give Zakat,
> Will have their reward
> With their Lord:
> On them shall be no fear,
> Nor shall they grieve.

Zakat is the regular and obligatory charity in an organised Muslim community, usually 10 per cent on the fruits of the earth; 2.5 per cent of merchandise, including gold and silver; and up to 24 camels, the payable *zakat* is one sheep or goat for every 5 camels; up to 60-69 cows the payable *zakat* is 2 cows of one-year old; and up to 40-120 sheep or goats, the payable *zakat* is one sheep or one goat. (I am indebted to Dr Mayanja for this information.) Detailed rules are laid down in the texts (see, e.g., Malik, 1982:119-135) as to the properties on which *zakat* is to be levied, and there are certain differences in this between the various schools of Islamic law, the percentage payable and also regarding the purposes to which the proceeds are to be dedicated. Zakat should not be confused with *sadaqa* – recommendable alms, which are given in Allah's name, mainly to the poor and needy, and for cognate purposes. Their neglect is not punished by God, but their performance is rewarded.

The proceeds from *zakat* are to be given to the poor and the needy and those who are employed to administer the funds. *Zakat* funds are not to be diverted to other uses. Besides ordinary indigents, there are certain classes of people whose need is great and should be relieved. These include (Islamic Researches, 1992: commentary no 1320) (1) men who have been weaned from hostility to Islam, who would probably be persecuted by their former associates, and require assistance until they establish new connections in their new environment; (2) those in bondage, literally and figuratively: captives of war must be redeemed, slaves should be helped to freedom to develop their own gifts; (3) those who are held in the grip of debt should be helped to economic freedom; (4) those who are struggling and striving in Allah's cause by teaching or fighting or in duties assigned to them by the Islamic state, who are thus unable to earn their ordinary livelihood; and (5) strangers stranded on the way. All these people have a claim to charity.

Zakat is thus given to the poor, in order to spare them the humiliation of poverty; to the humble, in order to strengthen their position in the community; to the collectors of *zakat*, to reward them for their good work; to slaves, in order to help them regain their freedom; to those who are used to it, so that they would not turn against the *Ummah* and weaken its unity; and finally, it is given for the sake of jihad in order to make the word of Allah triumph. The categories of beneficiaries for whom *zakat* is prescribed in the Qur'an (Surah 9: 60) are the neediest categories of the community. This means that the prescription of *zakat* aims at ensuring the welfare of the *Ummah* as a whole, by ridding it of poverty and indigence.

The Muslims' obligation to pay *zakat* to the legal beneficiaries takes various forms, which are shown in reasonable graduation: one's kith and kin; orphans; people who are in real need but who never ask; the people who ask and are entitled to ask; and the slaves – Muslims must also do all they can to give or buy slaves' freedom.

Indeed in various verses the Qur'an emphasises the righteousness of paying *zakat* for the ransom of slaves. Slavery takes many insidious forms and all are included.

Zakat is the third pillar of the five pillars of Islam, and the other four are: to testify that Muhammad is God's prophet and messenger; to establish five daily prayers; to fast during the month of Ramadhan; and lastly to go on the Hajj for those with material and financial ability to do so. In some Muslim lands *zakat* is collected and disbursed by the government, while in others, e.g. Uganda, it is left to the conscience of the individual. It is clear from *Surah* 2: 277 that the command for the Muslims to pay *zakat* to the legal beneficiaries makes it obligatory on the Muslims who are sufficiently blessed with Allah's bounty.

Considering that the Qur'an commands Muslims to give *zakat;* and

Considering also that Muslims who are liable to give *zakat*, but fail to do so, are in breach of the Qur'anic injunction;

It is obvious, then, that Muslims have an inescapable obligation to fulfil the third pillar of their faith, i.e. to pay *zakat*. From this obligation, then, arises the Muslims' right to pay *zakat* without let or hindrance from the government. It should be kept in view that the Muslim community as a whole is responsible for the welfare and protection of the weak, the poor, and the needy in its midst and usually it relies on the proceeds from *zakat* to meet this obligation. Indeed, proceeds from *zakat* are a major source of income for religious groups which, as we noted in Chapter 1, meet social needs left unattended by state bureaucracies.

Within an Islamic banking system, *zakat* and *sadaqa* funds could be mobilised and channelled through an Islamic bank for investment in poverty - reduction projects. It is such funds that some of the new emerging economic power houses in East Asia – Malaysia and

Indonesia – have invested in their industrial take-off. It is high time that the government enacted the necessary legislation to make it possible for those interested in setting up Islamic banks in the country to do so to facilitate the investment of *zakat* and *sadaqa* funds in an interest - free economy.

The Right to Acquire Education

No definition of education and no clarification of its aims is possible unless the nature of man and the significance of knowledge are first made clear. Man, according to Islam, is composed of soul and body, with the soul being rational and the body animal; he is at once spirit and matter; he is a unity as an individual and his individuality is referred to as the self; he is endowed with attributes bestowed by God. Man possesses spiritual and rational organs of cognition such as the heart and the intellect, and faculties relating to physical, intellectual and spiritual vision, experience and consciousness. He is forgetful by nature and inclined towards injustice and ignorance. His most important gift is knowledge which pertains to spiritual as well as intelligible and tangible realities. Knowledge must guide him towards a high ultimate destiny in the hereafter which is determined by how he conducts himself in this world.

Islam is a special body of knowledge granted to man by God, who is the source of all knowledge. Knowledge is a trust which must be borne with responsibility and justice and wisdom with reference to man and nature. In nature are found (Ali, 1987:41) signs of knowledge which must be approached in reverential humility and with purity of purpose.

Considering that Islam offers man a complete code of life in the Qur'an and *Sunna* which, if followed wholeheartedly, leads man towards the realisation of the greatest glory that God has reserved for him as *Khalifatullah* (God's viceroy on earth);

Considering also that in order to follow the code of Islam adequately and attain a consciousness of himself as the *Khalifatullah*, man needs training from his childhood, both at home and in the society in which he lives, and that this training should be of his total personality, his spirit, intellect, and rational self, imagination and bodily senses, and not one part at the expense of others;

Considering further that his faith in the code and practice according to this faith are possible only when the training is so organised that all other aspects of his personality are dominated by his spiritual self, which alone can receive and strengthen faith, develop his will-power and lead man to good deeds and salvation;

Considering finally that in view of the fact that, though all Muslim countries teach Islam as one of the many subjects, they have not as yet substituted anti-Islamic concepts with Islamic ones, it is essential to reclassify knowledge and reorganise education;

It is, therefore, imperative that:

1. Education should aim at the balanced growth of the total personality of man through the training of man's spirit, intellect, rational self, feelings and bodily senses. The training imparted to a Muslim must be such that faith is infused into the whole of his personality and creates in him an emotional attachment to Islam and enables him to follow the Quar'an and the *Sunna* and be governed by the Islamic system of values willingly and joyfully so that he may proceed to the realisation of his status as the *Khalifatullah* to whom God has promised the authority of the universe.

2. Education by precept and example should instill piety and encourage self-purification as a means of penetrating the deep mysteries of the universe and opening the heart to the fear and love of God.

3. Education should promote in man the creative impulse to rule himself and the universe as a true servant of God, not by opposing and coming into conflict with Nature but by understanding its laws and harnessing its forces for the growth of a personality that is in harmony with it. (These aims of education are adopted from Ali, 1987:41-43.)

Thus, the most important objective of Islamic education is the completest possible exposure of the child (boy or girl) to the life-giving words of the Qur'an, without which the child would have no hope of happiness in this world or salvation in the next. Closely linked with this is instruction in the prayers and other formal duties of Islam. And, considering that the Muslim community as a whole is responsible for the protection of the weak, the poor, and the needy, the state should train people for work so that they can satisfy their primary needs. Indeed, Qutb contends (see Moussalli, 1999:147) that Islam considers acquiring education with which one can earn one's livelihood a duty of every Muslim. The community has a responsibility to facilitate the fulfilment of this duty, however.

Ignorance is the most important factor that gives rise to man's failure to resort to reason and his *fitra* (innate disposition). The fact that a man without beneficial learning and education lacks a sense of reasoning and discrimination, weakens his consciousness and enfeebles his good and noble propensities, and leads himself more easily towards the wrong path. It is believed in Islam that the real protection from vice can only be provided through possessing 'Divine Knowledge'. For this reason, Islam has undertaken the task of fighting illiteracy and ignorance by propagating the means of learning and education which promote the foundation for a peaceful and prosperous reconstruction. This particular emphasis on education (The Shaiat, Oct. 1994:8) stems from Islam's belief that the absence of 'good knowledge' helps to let loose the forces of vice and evil, while possessing 'good and constructive knowledge' blesses man with the light of wisdom and perception and helps 'to set faith in him, springs of love, mercy and beauty, and confirms the desire to reject any aspect of evil'. The crucial role of education in Islam is attested to by a well-known prayer in the Qur'an (Surah 20: 114): 'O Lord, increase me in knowledge.' Furthermore, Prophet Muhammad said that Allah has created nothing to be compared in excellence to reason – reason being the essence of knowledge.

However, modern secular schools are only partly concerned with moral values. The teachers are concerned to develop to the fullest possible extent the reasoning power, the talents, and the skills of all pupils. To them the good is not the student who is good in any moral sense but the student who has assimilated their instructions to their satisfaction. There are countless teachers throughout the world whose care for their students goes beyond such concentration on value-free instruction. But such devotion to the moral welfare of their pupils is all too often an optional extra. Many teachers indeed are embarrassed by the suggestion that there is a moral dimension to the practice of their professional skills. Challenged about this, some will take refuge in the view that the moral welfare of school children is a matter for their parents and for their religious leaders. To the Muslim, from the time of Prophet Muhammad himself until the present day, such an attitude is nothing short of impiety. In a word, (Abdurrahman and Canham, 1978:70:71), Islam cannot reconcile itself to a view of education which lacks a spiritual dimension and fails to place moral values at the very heart and centre of learning.

Indeed, it is now being increasingly realised that modern secular education is both against the Islamic philosophy of life and ill-suited to the practical requirements of the Muslim societies. Muslims view the concept of modern secular education as a hollow concept, which lays too much emphasis on objectivity and neutrality, and cares little about its usefulness to society. It is clear from the foregoing observations that modern secular education runs contrary to the Islamic spirit which guides the entire outlook of the faithful.

Against this background, it is quite obvious that Muslim parents have an inescapable duty and responsibility and, therefore, a right to ensure that their offspring are facilitated to acquire good quality Islamic education; or else they risk being condemned for failing to carry out their parental and religious obligations. And, as shown later in Chapter 5, Muslims in the former European colonies in Africa, including Uganda, have every reason to believe that the so-called modern secular education is pernicious to the welfare of the *Ummah*.

The Right to Marry Four Wives and to Divorce by Repudiation

The Right to Marry Four Wives

Polygamy is a feature closely associated with sexual promiscuity among Africans generally and with Islam in the Western mind. The passage authorising polygamy is one of the most controversial in the entire text. The Qur'an says (Surah 4:3):

> If ye fear that ye shall not
> Be able to deal justly
> With the orphans,
> Marry women of your choice,
> Two, or three, or four;
> But if ye fear that ye shall not
> Be able to deal justly (with them),
> Then only one, or
> That which your right hands possess.
> That will be more suitable,
> To prevent you
> From doing injustice.

The prescription is usually taken to mean no man should marry more than four wives. It then limits rather than introduces the plurality of spouses. It may, however, be taken as encouraging men with only one wife to marry as many as three other wives. Certain modern reformers put an entirely different interpretation on the passage, arguing that, since absolute justice cannot be maintained by a husband with four wives, the intent of the injunction is monogamous marriage.

The prescription reminds us of the immediate occasion which proceeded its promulgation. It was after the battle of Uhud, when the Muslim community was left with many orphans, widows and some captives (women). Their treatment was to be governed by principles of the greatest humanity and equality. The unrestricted number of wives of the 'times of ignorance' was now strictly limited to a maximum of four, provided one 'could treat them with perfect equality in material things as well as in affection'. Yusuf

Ali further contends (Yusuf Ali, 1973: Commentary no. 509) that 'as this condition is most difficult to fulfil I understand the recommendation to be towards monogamy'. But to-date this view remains unacceptable to the generality of Muslims, particularly men. A more generally accepted view in the mainstream Sunni Islam is that a man can marry a maximum of four wives provided he can treat them justly in material things as well as in affection.

Thus in Islam polygamy is permissible but not commanded. It is, therefore, not obligatory on every Muslim man. Rather, it is conditional on a man's ability to treat his wives with justice in material things as well as in affection. And, whether or not a Muslim man marries one wife or four wives, is strictly his personal preference. But marrying up to four wives is a right to which Muslim men are justly entitled. Small wonder, then, that Muslim men, the world over, believe that it is their right to marry up to four wives! So, if a Muslim man chooses to marry more than one wife, it is his right to do so, and no man-made law can legitimately deny him this right. But he could as well choose to marry one wife which is also within his rights.

The Right to Divorce by Repudiation

Islam recognises marriage as a contract between two individuals who can legally break the contract. And all schools of Islamic law recognise that a marriage may be terminated extrajudicially, either by the husband exercising his power of *talaq* (divorce by repudiation) or by mutual consent. But they differ radically as to the grounds upon which it may be terminated by a judicial decree. This controversy is beyond the scope of the present study, however. Here our concern is with divorce by repudiation which Muslim men regard as their religio-social right. Under orthodox Islamic law divorce can be effected in three ways (see Coulson, 1969:45):

1. By mutual consent of spouses, where the agreement of the parties dissolves the union without the necessity of any recourse to judicial proceedings.

2. By a judicial decree of divorce granting the petition of a wife who establishes that her husband is afflicted with a disease of mind or body, or is guilty of some matrimonial offence such as cruelty, or desertion.

3. By unilateral termination of the marriage by the husband exercising his right of *talaq* (repudiation). It is arbitrary and absolute. The husband may exercise it at will and his motive in doing so is not subject to scrutiny by the court or any other official body.

Triple repudiation has become the normal form of divorce. A repudiation or a divorce repeated three times constitutes a final and irrevocable dissolution of the marriage. The husband ought to pronounce three separate repudiations or divorces during three successive states of purity from menstruation of his wife. The Qur'an does not specify the grounds for divorce, however. It says (Surah 2:228), for example:

> Divorced women
> Shall wait concerning themselves
> For three monthly periods.
> And it is not lawful for them
> To hide what Allah
> Hath created in their wombs,
> If they have faith
> In Allah and the Last Day.
> And their husbands
> Have the better right
> To take them back
> In that period, if
> They wish for reconciliation.
> And women shall have rights
> Similar to the rights
> Against them, according
> To what is equitable;
> But men have a degree
> Over them
> And Allah is Exalted in Power, wise.

The Qur'an further says (Surah 2:229):

> A divorce is only
> Permissible twice; after that,
> The parties should either hold
> Together on equitable terms,
> Or separate with kindness.
> It is not lawful for you,
> (Men), to take back
> Any of your gifts (from your wives),
> Except when both parties
> Fear that they would be
> Unable to keep the limits
> Ordained by Allah
> If ye (judges) do indeed
> Fear that they would be
> Unable to keep the limits
> Ordained by Allah,
> There is no blame on either
> Of them if she give
> Something for her freedom
> These are the limits
> Ordained by Allah;
> So do not transgress them
> If any do transgress
> The limits ordained by Allah,
> Such persons wrong
> (Themselves as well as others).

The Qur'an also says (Surah 2:230):

> So if a husband
> Divorces his wife (irrevocably),
> He cannot, after that,
> Re-marry her until
> After she has married
> Another husband and
> He has divorced her.
> In that case there is
> No blame on either of them
> If they re-unite, provided
> They feel that they

> Can keep the limits
> Ordained by Allah.
> Such are the limits
> Ordained by Allah,
> Which He makes plain
> To those who know.

The termination of a marriage bond is a very serious matter, not only for the family concerned, but also for society as a whole. Hence every lawful device which can equitably re-unite those who have previously lived together is approved, provided that there is mutual love between the parties and that they can live on honourable terms with each other. If these conditions are fulfilled, it is not right for outsiders to prevent or hinder the reunion.

Islam tries to maintain the married state as far as possible, especially where children are concerned, by encouraging reconciliation between the parties that are due to divorce. The aim is to check hasty action, as far as possible, and leave the door to reconciliation open at many stages even after divorce. Firstly, after double pronouncement of *talaq* (repudiation), a period of waiting (*iddat*) for three monthly courses is prescribed, in order to see if the marriage, now conditionally dissolved, is likely to result in offspring. However, this condition is not necessary where the divorced woman is a virgin.

However, two divorces (double pronouncement of *talaq*) followed by reunion are permissible. The husband may retract and revoke the two divorces at will during the wife's *iddat*. Therefore, if the husband wishes to resume marital relations, he need not wait for the end of his wife's *iddat*. But if he does not so wish, she is free to marry someone else after her *iddat*. However, if a man takes back his wife after two divorces, he must do so only on equitable terms, i.e. he must not put pressure on the woman to prejudice her rights in any way and they must live clean lives, respecting each other's responsibilities. The Qur'an in *Surah* 2 verse 231 gives two conditional clauses (1) 'when ye divorce women', and (2) 'when they fulfil their *iddat*': followed by two consequential clauses, (3) take them back on equitable terms, or (4) set them free with kindness.

The third pronouncement of *talaq* makes the divorce irrevocable, until the woman marries some other man and he divorces her. This is to set an almost impossible condition for the reunion after the third divorce. The lesson is (Yusuf Ali, 1992: Commentary no. 260): if a man loves a woman, he should not allow a sudden gust of temper or anger to induce him to take hasty and thoughtless action.

If a separation is inevitable, a man is not allowed to ask back for any gifts or property he may have given to his wife. This is for the protection of the economically weaker sex. Lest this protective provision works against the woman's freedom, an exception to the rule is prescribed. The prohibitions and limits cited here are in the interests of good and honourable lives for both the husband and the wife, and in the interests of a good society, without either private or public scandals. But, if there is any fear that in safeguarding her economic rights, her very freedom of person may suffer as a result of the husband's refusal to dissolve the marriage, or perhaps by treating her with cruelty, then, in such exceptional cases, it is permissible for the wife to give some material consideration to the husband. But the need and equity of such material consideration should be decided by a properly constituted and impartial court.

The Qur'an also commands that husbands who wish to take their wives back after they have fulfilled their *iddat* should do so, and on equitable terms. They, should not however, take them back (Yusuf Ali, 1992: commentary no. 262) 'to injure them or to take undue advantage of them.' 'Let no one think,' Yusuf Ali observes, 'that the liberty given to him can be used for his own selfish ends.' 'If he uses the law to injure the weaker party [i.e., the wife], his own moral and spiritual nature suffers'.

And, although the man has a right to divorce his wife or wives by repudiation, it is quite clear from the 'prohibitions and limits' discussed here that his right must be exercised with the utmost care, if one is not to transgress these 'prohibitions and limits' which, as the Qur'an tells us, were 'ordained by Allah, so that those who transgress them earn themselves Allah's wrath'. Also, the fact that in cases of divorce by repudiation, a man is not allowed to ask back for any gifts or property he may have given to his wife, except in exceptional cases, acts as a powerful economic limitation of his freedom to repudiate his wife or wives.

Equally significant in restricting a man's freedom to repudiate the marriage of his wife is the fact that, after the third divorce or repudiation, a man is not permitted to re-marry his ex-wife until she marries some other man and he in turn divorces her! An impossible condition, one might say. It is intended to intervene in situations where divorce for mutual incompatibility is allowed, that might encourage parties to act hastily, then repent, and again wish to separate, thus resulting in capricious divorce repeatedly. This prohibition ensures that, if a man loves a woman, he does not allow 'a sudden gust of temper or anger' to influence him to take a hasty action in a serious matter such as divorce. So, after the two divorces, the parties must definitely make up their minds, either to dissolve their marriage permanently, or to live honourable lives together in love and mutual respect. However, the institution of *talaq* stands out in the whole range of family law as occasioning the gravest prejudice to the status of Muslim women.

Despite the Qur'an's definite assurance that men and women are equal before the law, the legal position of the wife under a system of polygamy, and *talaq*, is obviously less favourable than that of the husband. Nonetheless, the Qur'an (*Surah* 4:19) commands Muslim men to live with their wives 'on a footing of kindness and equality'.

5

Ugandan Muslims' Perception of the Rights of Muslims

An Introductory Comment

The data analysed in this chapter was collected from Sunni Muslims for reasons stated earlier. The chief aim of the analysis presented here is to assess the level of Ugandan Muslims' awareness of the religio-political rights of orthodox Muslims, and to establish, whether or not, there is a correlation between one's level of educational attainment and one's perception of these rights. The analysis deals only with the principal religio-political rights common to the four Muslim sects in Uganda, and between which there are no major doctrinal differences. Therefore, although the conclusions reached are tentative, nevertheless they are applicable to the entire mainstream of the Muslim population in Uganda.

This chapter also discusses very briefly the basis of the legitimacy of Islamic legislation that makes it distinguishable from un-Islamic legislation, i.e. laws made without reference to Islamic principles and which do not conform to Islamic teachings. Here it is emphasised that in Islamic legislation the legitimacy of laws is derived from God. And, for a law to command the respect and obedience of Muslims, it ought to adhere to this axiom.

The Right to be Ruled by a Fellow Muslim

Fifty-two respondents, representing 85 percent, listed 'God-fearing' as one of the four finest qualities of 'a good political leader'. And since the same respondents also indicated that the main functions of the state were to rule in accordance with Islamic principles and to promote Islam, it can be safely concluded that 'God-fearing' explicitly implies 'being a believer', i.e. a Muslim. This is because the only God that Muslims fear and love is Allah and not any other god. Indeed (Yusuf Ali, 1973: commentary no. 177), a righteous and 'God fearing' man should not only obey salutary relations, but he should also fix his gaze on the love of Allah and the love of his fellow men. His faith should be true and sincere; he must be prepared to show it in deeds of charity to his fellow men; he must be a good citizen, supporting social organisations; and his own soul must be firm and unshaken in all circumstances. And sixty-three respondents, representing 90 percent, listed 'an educated Muslim' among the four finest qualities of a good religio-political leader.

It can be surmised from this analysis that the generality of the Muslim population in Uganda are aware of their right to be ruled by a fellow Muslim. Similarly, they are also aware that ideally the main goals of an Islamic state are to 'promote Islam, safeguard Islamic principles, and to ensure justice for the citizenry, and to keep peace and security' which, from the Muslims' perspective, can best be achieved under the sharia.

The Right to be Ruled in Accordance with the Sharia

When asked to describe a 'just world', 50 respondents, representing 71 percent, described it either as a place 'where the sharia reigns supreme', or where there is justice based on the sharia, or 'the world ruled in accordance with the sharia'. The other 20 respondents, representing 29 per cent, indicated that they did not know what constituted a 'just world'.

But when asked whether or not the sharia legal system should be immediately introduced in Uganda, 34 respondents, representing 49 percent, were not in favour of the immediate introduction of the sharia legal system in Uganda. Among the reasons given for this stance were the following:

1. The Muslim population in Uganda is still a very small minority.

2. Most Muslims, including some sheikhs, are not knowledgeable about the sharia and, as such, the country lacks learned sheikhs to administer the sharia.

3. Uganda does not have a Muslim president.

Interestingly, 13 respondents out of the 18 with either diploma or university degree qualifications were among those who rejected the idea of immediate introduction of the sharia in Uganda.

However, 14 respondents out of 20 with neither western nor Islamic education supported the immediate introduction of the sharia while only six respondents, representing 30 percent of this group, opposed it. The main reasons given for this response included the following:

1. Muslims must be governed by the sharia.

2. The sharia can bring about peace in Uganda.

3. The sharia is divine law and universal.

4. The sharia is the only guarantee of justice.

5. The sharia will solve the problems of corruption and immorality.

Out of the ten respondents with some Islamic education eight, representing 80 percent, supported immediate introduction of the sharia legal system in Uganda, while the other two, representing 20 percent, opposed it. This would seem to suggest that the idea of immediate introduction of the sharia legal system in Uganda is more popular with poorly educated Muslims and less popular with Muslims with higher education, particularly Western education.

The main reason for these divergent opinions is the inability of the Muslims with little formal education to appreciate the intricacies involved in the implementation of the sharia in a country like Uganda which is predominantly Christian.

But even the respondents who rejected the idea of the immediate introduction of the sharia legal system in Uganda, did appreciate the fact that ultimately, when conditions become auspicious for an Islamic state, the sharia legal system should be introduced since Muslims are required by the Qur'an to adhere to the sharia.

In the light of the foregoing analysis, there is little doubt that there is a correlation between one's level of education and one's perception of the Muslims' right to be governed in accordance with the sharia.

The Right to Say the Five Canonical Prayers and to Attend the Jumu'a Prayer

Fifty respondents, representing 71 percent, listed 'praying five times a day', at prescribed times, as part of the Muslims' right of worship. Of course, this includes attendance of the Jumu'a Friday prayer. Those among the respondents who were in salaried employment pointed out that non-Muslim employers did not provide places of worship on their premises. They also complained that they were not given time off to pray at the prescribed times while at work.

When asked whether or not Friday should be made a non-working day for Muslim employees, 34 respondents, representing 48 percent, answered in the affirmative. The reasons given in support of this stance, among others, were that:

1. Friday is a public holiday recognised in Islam.

2. Friday is to Muslims what Sunday is to Christians.

3. Friday should be made a public holiday to enable Muslims to attend the Jumu'a prayer.

On the other hand 25 respondents, representing 36 percent, answered in the negative. The reasons given in support of this stance were that:

1. The Qur'an encourages Muslims to work after Jumu'a prayer.

2. It was uncalled for to make Friday a public holiday since the Jumu'a prayer takes a very short time.

3. In Islam there is no holy day on which people should not work.
4. Islam discourages laziness and encourages hard work.

Instead, they proposed that Muslim employees should be given adequate time off to attend the Jumu'a prayer and return to work as recommended by the Qur'an. To them, so long as adequate time for the Jumu'a prayer was provided, there was no need to make Friday a non-working day.

Eleven respondents, representing 16 percent, were undecided. Of the 18 respondents with either university degree or diploma qualifications 12, or 67 percent, were in favour of keeping Friday a working day while six, or 33 percent, were in favour of making it a non-working day for Muslims only. But 15 respondents out of the 20 respondents without any formal education were in favour of making Friday a non-working day for Muslims only, while of this group only five respondents representing 25 percent, were in favour of keeping Friday a working day. The opinion among the 10 respondents with some Islamic education was almost evenly divided, with 6 being in favour of keeping Friday a working day and 4 being in favour of making it a non-working day for Muslim employees only.

The conclusion that can be drawn from this analysis is that Muslims with higher education, particularly Islamic education, are less likely to be ardent protagonists of a non-working Friday since, from their knowledge of the Qur'an, they would know that the Muslims' duty to attend the Jumu'a prayer does not absolve them from their earthly duty 'to seek of Allah's bounty'. This argument is strengthened by the fact that, whereas the reasons given above by the opponents of a non-working Friday conform to the Qur'anic injunctions, those given by its protagonists are far-fetched and quite misleading. And, as stated previously, many Islamic countries which have decreed Friday a public holiday have done so in response to socio-economic needs rather than to meet a religious obligation per se. Thus there is a correlation between one's level of education, particularly Islamic education, and one's perception of the Muslim's right to have a non-working Friday, and by inference one's perception of the Muslims' right to attend the Jumu'a prayer on Friday. It is quite true, however, that the current working practices in most work-places, both in the public sector and the private sector, and educational institutions, neither provide places for worship nor give Muslims adequate time to attend the Jumu'a prayer.

The Right to Wage a Jihad of the Sword

In special circumstances the jihad of the sword, i.e. war, is lawful and a religious duty for upright and conscientious Muslims. The special circumstances under which the jihad of the sword is lawful were discussed in Chapter 2. When asked to list the conditions that constitute an ideal situation for waging a lawful jihad of the sword, 50 respondents, representing 71 per cent, listed the following conditions which in their view justify the declaration of a lawful jihad:

1. If oppression and monopoly of power on the part of the ruling party becomes a fact and a distinct political class takes shape in the form of a tribe–based party, which monopolises state power and wealth, whereas the majority of the people are deprived of these things so much so that the state becomes the private property of the ruling party.
2. If behavioural deviation becomes a social phenomenon whereby corruption creeps steadily into public life and its symptoms appear in both individual and group behaviour.
3. If Muslims are oppressed, persecuted and prevented from spreading Islam by the state.
4. If Muslims are denied freedom of worship.
5. If a non-Muslim state wages war on an Islamic state.
6. If non-Muslims in an Islamic state refuse to give up unbelief and embrace Islam.

7. If the authenticity of the Qur'an is denied and no remorse is forthcoming.

The above conditions cover adequately those discussed in Chapter 2. Of course, the danger is that, more often than not, these conditions are often interpreted differently by the people concerned. This means that there is no uniformity in the way in which Muslims of different schools of thought or sects would react to any of these conditions. But they clearly show that the generality of Ugandan Muslims are quite aware of the conditions that can justify the declaration of a jihad of the sword in self-defence or in self-preservation.

Indeed, about 35 percent of the respondents cited the freedom of the Muslim community to elect its leaders, particularly the Mufti (one who issues religious edicts (*fata'wa*: singular-*fatwa*) in a Muslim community, or leader of the Muslim community), as the Muslims' right of worship'. Thus, any involvement of a non-Islamic government, such as that of Uganda, in the election of the Muslim leaders is deemed as interference and an infringement upon the Muslims' right of worship, which in extreme cases would justify the declaration of an armed jihad. It is hardly surprising, then, that on various occasions (see, e.g., Kanyeihamba, 1998) in the recent past some Muslim leaders have publicly called upon the NRM government to stop its alleged interference in Muslims' affairs.

The consensus among the respondents was that the government should leave Muslims alone to settle their problems through the use of the sharia. This does not come as a complete surprise, however. A sizeable section of the Muslim population believe that Muslims in Uganda have been oppressed and treated as third-class citizens by every government before and since the overthrow of Idi Amin's government in 1979. They also believe that these governments have sponsored divisions among Muslims in order to keep the Muslim community backward.

The Right to Pay *Zakat*

Zakat, as earlier stated, is the third pillar of Islam. Muslims who are liable to pay it, but fail to do so, are in breach of Qur'anic injunctions. In some Muslim countries *zakat* is collected, and disbursed, by the state, while in others, such as Uganda, it is left to the conscience of the individual. However, in Uganda today, the overwhelming majority of Muslims do not pay *zakat* as would be expected of them. When asked why this was so, the following responses were obtained:

1. Sixty respondents, who included the 18 subjects with higher education, representing 85 percent, blamed the present laxity in paying *zakat* on Ugandan Muslims' ignorance about this third pillar of Islam.

2. Fifty-five respondents, representing 78 percent, stated that *zakat* is not paid by the majority of Muslims in Uganda because it is often confused with *sadaqa*. (*Sadaqa* is a gift made to obtain a heavenly reward and it cannot be revoked.)

3. Fifty-three respondents, representing 75 percent, stated that the majority of Muslims in Uganda do not pay *zakat* because the Muslim community lacks well qualified and honest sheikhs to assess it. *Zakat* is a definite portion of one's wealth.

4. Forty-three respondents, representing 61 percent, imputed the present laxity in paying *zakat* to the alleged rapacious behaviour of the current Muslim leaders in the country which manifests itself in rampant embezzlement and corruption.

5. Thirty-five respondents, representing 50 percent, blamed today's laxity in paying *zakat* on the Muslims' poverty allegedly resulting from overtaxation by government.

6. Sixteen respondents, representing 23 percent, stated that a majority of Uganda Muslims do not pay *zakat* owing to the multiplicity of Muslim factions which would make the utilisation of the proceeds from *zakat* very problematic indeed.

7. A small fraction of the respondents (5), representing 7 percent, imputed the current laxity in paying *zakat* by Muslims in Uganda to the absence of an Islamic state.

The information obtained from the respondents would seem to suggest that today the majority of Muslims in Uganda who are liable to pay *zakat* do not do so, either because they are ignorant of it, or because they genuinely confuse it with *sadaqa*, or because they lack well qualified and honest sheikhs to assess it, or because they fear that their leaders would embezzle the proceeds from *zakat*. Since it was generally agreed among the respondents that a majority of the Muslim population who are liable to pay *zakat* do not usually do so for one or more of these reasons, and since none of these reasons is commended by the Qur'an, it can be concluded that the generality of Muslims' perception of 'the right to pay *zakat*' is still very low.

Indeed, when asked to suggest two remedial measures to the current laxity in paying *zakat*, 57 respondents, representing 81.4 percent, suggested that Muslims should be made more aware of the religious importance and significance of *zakat* through seminars, conferences, and sermons by the Imams (prayer-leaders). The second popular suggestion, which was made by 47 respondents, representing 67 percent, was that the government should reduce taxes on Muslims so that many more Muslims could have sufficient income from which to pay *zakat*. It should also be noted that in countries where the sharia is the law of the land, *zakat* is the only income tax payable to the state by Muslims. Thus, if Muslims in Uganda were to pay taxes to the government like any other citizen and to pay *zakat* to Muslim authorities as well, they would be liable to double taxation. Yet today most Muslims are penurious in common with other Ugandans, so that only very few of them could afford to pay double taxation. It is quite clear from our discussion on the assessment of *zakat* in Chapter 4 that only a small percentage of the Muslims population in the country today are liable to pay *zakat*.

The Right to Acquire Education

In order to follow the code of Islam adequately and attain a consciousness of himself as the viceroy of Allah on earth, man needs training from his childhood, both at home and in the society in which he lives. This training should be of his total personality, his spirit, intellect, and rational self, imagination and bodily senses, and not of one part at the expense of others. It is quite clear, therefore, that the type of education currently given in our schools, especially primary schools, does not meet this criterion, at any rate, for Muslim children.

Thus, when asked whether or not they were satisfied with the present type of primary education, especially as regards religious and moral instruction for Muslim children attending non-Muslim founded primary schools, 58 respondents, representing 83 percent, expressed dissatisfaction with it. It was reasoned that the present education system, particularly primary education, was bad for Muslims, on the grounds that:

1. Islam and Arabic language are not taught.
2. Qur'anic studies are not incorporated in the examinable school syllabus and, as such, they are neglected.
3. Government does not employ Qur'anic and Arabic teachers to cater for the religious education of Muslim pupils.
4. Primary education lacks a moral content.
5. Muslim pupils are not given time to pray five times a day at prescribed times.

Twelve respondents, representing 17 percent, expressed satisfaction with the type of primary education presently given in government-aided primary schools on the grounds that it caters for both secular and religious education. This is not necessarily true of Muslim children attending these schools, however. And since the 12 respondents were among those without any formal education, it can be surmised that their approval of the type of education given in government-aided primary schools today reflects their lack of understanding of what goes on in schools and perhaps their little understanding of the Islamic faith.

The Islamic concept of life, as envisaged in the Qur'an, is that man should devote his entire life to the cause of Allah. This being the case, his education, especially during childhood (see, e.g., Fafunwa, 1974:50 -72), must give top priority to Islam and Arabic language. But the current primary school curriculum does not give priority to Islamic studies. Instead, it is oriented towards secularism. And, from the Muslims' point of view, an education which does not emphasise Islamic studies, like Uganda's primary education, is not capable of inculcating moral values. To Muslims, only Islamic education is well suited to build morals. The Prophet Muhammad stated in one of his sayings, for example, that 'I have been sent only for the purpose of perfecting good morals' (see, e.g., Malik, 1982: 438). Thus, from the Muslims' point of view, worshipping God and practising the five pillars of Islam is part of building personal character and morals.

In fact, in September 2000, the then Assistant Commissioner for Primary Education, Mr Ahmed Kamya, who, as his name indicates, is a Muslim, exalted Kamwokya Islamic Primary School for teaching both Islamic and secular education because, as he put it, 'the Qur'anic teachings shape the morals of pupils' (*The Monitor*, 5 Sept. 2000: 11). From the Muslims' point of view, the type of primary education currently given in our primary schools lacks a moral content, since it does not emphasise Islamic education, especially Qur'anic studies. Instead, it is an education with no moral content as pointed out by the overwhelming majority of the respondents and, therefore, not good enough for Muslim children whose education ordinarily should prepare them for happiness in this world and salvation in the next.

It can thus be concluded that the present educational system denies Muslim parents their right to give their children an education that befits Muslim children and that would instil piety and encourage self-purification as a means of penetrating the deep mysteries of the universe and opening the heart to the fear and love of God. The fact that all the respondents with higher education rejected the type of education currently given in our primary schools as inappropriate for Muslim children, while all the respondents who approved of it were those without any formal education, would seem to suggest a correlation between one's level of educational attainment and his perception of the Muslims' right to acquire good quality education for their children.

It is imperative, therefore, that the Islamic-oriented institutions of higher education in the country should make a concerted efforts to implement programmes aimed at the Islamisation of the secular knowledge that is currently given in these institutions so as to make it palatable to Muslims. Islamisation of knowledge by definition is the act of injecting Islamic principles and perspectives into any piece of knowledge which was not originally based on *Tawhid* (belief in the oneness of God) as revealed to humankind in the Qur'an and the *Hadith*'. The Islamisation of knowledge, as Adamu (Adamu, 2001:2) tells us, 'is an aspect of the general Islamisation, which is a continuous act of a person always trying to align all his thoughts, actions, and skill with nothing but the provisions of the Islamic culture with the hope of obtaining Allah's pleasure and guidance in whatever it is he is doing'.

The promotion of the Islamisation of knowledge is also an act of war against secularism. Secularism, as Adamu (Adamu, 2001:1) has stated, 'is a doctrine in which religion is regarded as a personal affair of an individual and as such his other thoughts and actions should be separated from his religious activities'. This is quite contrary to Islamic philosophy and culture, where there is no action of man which is not regulated by the Islamic religion. Also, in Adamu's opinion (Adamu, 2001:2), in the fight against secularism in a multi-religious society, such as Ugandan society, the Islamisation of knowledge is the most effective weapon. In this respect, the Islamic University in Uganda (IUIU), which has been implementing a programme for the Islamisation of knowledge in the disciplines taught in the university since 1998, must be highly commended for its pioneering work and courage.

But until the secular education currently given in the country's institutions has been sufficiently Islamised, Muslim parents and their children alike will continue to view it with alarm and great suspicion since, from their point of view, its ultimate aim is to foster secularism that is inimical to Islam and Islamic culture. But, as Mika'ilu (Mika'ilu, (2002:7-15) has vividly shown, the Islamisation of knowledge in Uganda is bound to be arduous and time-consuming partly owing to the multi-religious nature of Ugandan society, and partly owing to the intractable problems currently facing the IUIU, such as inadequate funding and acute shortage of well-trained and competent academic staff, both of which have impeded, and continue to impede, the university's laudable efforts to fully implement its programme of the Islamisation of knowledge in its academic disciplines. Obviously, the IUIU, as the only Islamic university in the country mandated ' to ensure that Islamic culture is promoted in all the courses taught in the university', holds the key to the success of the Islamisation of knowledge, not only in Uganda, but also in the rest of East Africa. (For a comprehensive and authoritative discussion on the Islamisation of knowledge see, e.g., Islamic Thought, 1989.) However, this cannot be done without adequate resources. Nor is the process of Islamisation of knowledge in Uganda the responsibility of the IUIU alone. It is essential that other institutions of higher learning in the country, particularly Islamic-oriented ones, should do their bit in the task of Islamising knowledge in Uganda's education system.

The Legacy of Colonial Education

Our story on the Muslims' right to acquire education would not be complete if we did not comment on Muslims' justifiable fears and concerns regarding the so-called 'modern secular education' as practised in Uganda today. Western education as practised in Uganda today, and perhaps elsewhere in sub-Saharan Africa, is Christian-oriented and highly Westernised.

The Muslim population in Uganda have genuine concerns and fears in regarding the present education system in the country, not only as irrelevant to the educational needs of Muslim children and youth, but also as dangerous to the principles and teachings of Islam. The Islamic principles referred to here include, among others: integrity, sincerity, modesty, sacrifice, meditation and endeavour. Indeed, trustworthiness and sincerity are the two pillars of Islamic education. And, being the responsibility of the *ulama* (El-Mokhtar, tr. by El-Hakkouni, 1998:63), Islamic education should be delivered in good faith, and whoever fails to deliver it with due sincerity and honesty will have lied to the Prophet, with dire consequences. As its teachings have far-reaching effects on successive generations, Islamic education also determines the destiny of nations.

It is true that the welfare of a community depends on the efforts of each one of its members. But it is also true that the deeper the individual's awareness of his religious duties towards his community, the greater the results of his good works, for his own benefit and for the benefit of the community. Therefore, the main objective of Islamic education is to make every Muslim deeply aware of the fact that he is a member of the *Ummah* of Islam. Consequently, it is absolutely necessary that the individual Muslim understands, before anything else, and in consistency with the divine Qur'anic discourse, that the unity of the *Ummah* is of vital necessity. Hence, education of a Muslim child (El-Mokhtar, tr. by El-Hakkouni, 1998: 54) should start by studying the Qur'an, since it 'is the right way towards true guidance and, since Allah has invested the Qur'an with His divine light to guide whosoever He wills to the right path.' The early education of a Muslim child should also enable him to learn about the Prophet Muhammad. (On the aims of Islamic education see, e.g., Ali, 1986:41-44 and Fafunwa, 1974:50-72.)

The unity of the *Ummah* means that all members of the Muslim community are related one to the other to form a cohesive and coherent unit. This notion of solidarity clearly indicates that the strength of the community depends on the strength of its members, just as its weakness is due to the weakness of its members. In the light of this axiom El-Mokhtar tells us (El-Mokhtar, tr. by El-Hakkouni, 1998:53) thus:

> ... the believer understands that his duties are not limited to performing just those deeds for which he can get immediate reward. Rather, he must also commit himself to observing his duties towards his Creator, his own self, [his family], and his community. The ultimate goal behind his education in this fashion is to enable him to comply spontaneously, and as best as he could, with his Lord's Commands, and to avoid whatever is prohibited, except when compelled by necessity, neither craving nor transgressing; to make of him an individual Muslim who knows his obligation towards his Creator and endeavours to perform them; in short, a true believer who testifies that Allah is the Single Lord of the universe; that He is Unique; that He begot not, nor was He begotten; and that there is none equal to Him in His attributes; a believing Muslim who worships God as He deserves to be worshipped, yearning for His Mercy and fearing His Punishment.

By virtue of its moderate character, Islam is a religion that respects and gives equal importance to the rights of both the individual and the community. Thus, if educators give priority to the community in terms of education, they will not be minimising the rights of the individual, whereas if they give priority to the individual, the Muslim community will probably not achieve the required unity and cohesion, upon which depends the success of the Muslims' common action as can be learned from the previous quotation.

Therefore, an education, such as ours today, which we inherited from our former colonial rulers – the British – and which was originally intended to produce 'Westernised and detribalised Christian collaborators with the colonial rulers' (Tibenderana, 2003: esp. 171-174), and which gives priority to the individual – in terms of the curricula – at the expense of the community and, worse still, which relegates Islamic religious education – i.e. the Arabic language, the Qur'an, the Prophetic tradition, and the Islamic culture and civilisation to a peripheral position on the timetable even though these subjects form the solid foundation of education of every Muslim, cannot produce an ideal Muslim – 'the true believer' – who is envisaged in our previous quotation. Indeed

Uganda's education today is a continuation of the colonial education with only minor changes. But the framework of colonial education which was inherited at the time of Uganda's independence in 1962 from the British colonial rulers, or developed thereafter through imitation, are yet to undergo the slightest reform or change as regards the incorporation of Islamic religious education into the curricula of public education.

The Muslims' concerns and fears that today's education in the country constitutes the most serious hindrance to the progress of the *Ummah* and its development are well-founded and perhaps justified. For, as Ali tells us (Ali, 1986:38), 'it is now being increasingly realised that modern secular education is both against the Islamic philosophy of life and ill-suited to the practical requirements of the Muslim societies.' Speaking generally, Muslims view the concept of the so-called modern secular education as a hollow concept, which lays too much emphasis on objectivity and neutrality and cares little about its usefulness to society.

Not surprisingly the generality of the Muslim population in Uganda today regards the country's present education system as a threat to their way of life and to the welfare of the *Ummah* as a whole. No wonder they keep a wary eye on it. They are alarmed, for example, that:

1. The attendance of Muslim children and youths at Christian - founded schools and colleges, where the Christian culture still predominates, is most likely to weaken their faith.

2. Islamic religious subjects and the Arabic language are neglected in the school curriculum.

3. Government schools and colleges, which are attended by Muslim children and youths, do not often make provision in the timetable to allow their Muslim clientele to say the five canonical prayers at the specific periods and to attend the *Jumu'a* prayer without missing their lessons.

4. Government does not employ Muslim teachers of exemplary character and high calibre to teach Islamic religious subjects in government schools and colleges which are attended by Muslim students.

5. To date the government continues to ignore graduates of Islamic colleges in its recruitment policy to fill posts in the state bureaucracy and parastatals.

6. A majority of the teachers, especially male teachers, who teach in government schools and to whom Muslim girls who attend these schools are entrusted, lack good morals, thus making them a source of danger to these girls. Nor are female teachers in such schools of exemplary character to act as role models for the Muslim girls.

These are but a few of the difficulties with which Muslim parents in Uganda today have to contend with if they wish to give their children 'modern secular education'. A huge price indeed! One hopes that, sooner rather than later, the government will see the need to drastically reform the education system with a view to extirpating the major obstacles, such as the ones cited here, to the Muslims' acquisition of education. This should be done in the interest of the freedom of worship and religious co-existence, both of which are enshrined in the national constitution of 1995.

The times we live in are characterised by a boom in the domain of information, technology, and cultural exchanges and ramifications. Therefore, in order to move with the times, the Islamic *Ummah* should formulate new, adequate and relevant educational programmes so as to bring up the young generations in accordance with the principles and ethics of Islam, on the one hand, and to assume its human responsibility in the world of today by ensuring prosperity and glory for its individuals and groups, on the other. The Muslim leaders in the country should urgently and persistently pressurise the government to carry out a radical and comprehensive reform of the country's education system in order to achieve these goals. (On the proposed reforms of Islamic education which are deemed necessary to bring it into line with modernity see, e.g., El-Mokhtar, tr. by El-Harkkouni, 1998:105-142.)

The execution of the proposed 'radical and comprehensive reform' will not be easy. But then there are no easy solutions to the problem. The difficulty resides not in the conception of an ideal system of education, but rather in the deep-rooted habits and firmly established practices that characterise our present education system.

The Right to Marry Four Wives and to Divorce by Repudiation

Conditions for Muslim Marriage

The Qur'an, as we noted in Chapter 4, sets a limit to the number of wives a man can marry to four provided, of course, that he can treat them justly in material things as well as in affection. In addition, it lays down conditions which must be complied with by all those who wish to solemnise Muslim marriages.

1. Muslim men are forbidden to marry 'unbelieving women', i.e. pagan women, while Muslim women are forbidden to marry unbelieving men. Ordinarily, only a Muslim man and a Muslim woman, who are not forbidden to marry on the basis of either blood-relationships or 'milk-relationships' (fosterage), can contract a valid Muslim marriage under the sharia.

The Qur'an says (Surah 2:221), for example:

> Do not marry
> Unbelieving woman
> Until they believe:
> A slave woman who believes
> Is better than unbelieving woman
> Even though she allure you.
> Nor marry (your girls)
> To unbelievers until
> They believe:
> A man slave who believes
> Is better than an unbeliever.

2. A Muslim marriage requires some sort of dower or gift (*mahr*) for the wife. The Quran says in one instance (Surah 4:4), for example:

> And give the women
> (On marriage) their dower
> As an obligation; but if they
> Remit any part of it to you,
> Take it and enjoy it
> With right good cheer.

The Qur'an further says (Surah 2:36):

> But bestow on them
> (A suitable gift),
> The wealthy
> According to his means,
> And the poor
> According to his means;-
> Is due from those
> Who wish to do the right thing.

The indispensability of the dower or *mahr* to a Muslim marriage is further strengthened by another Qur'anic injunction (*Surah* 24:33) to the effect that a man who cannot afford marriage owing to lack of material means to provide a gift (*mahr*) for his prospective bride should keep himself chaste until God gives him the means out of His grace. It is no excuse for him to say that he must satisfy his natural cravings outside marriage. This must only happen within marriage.

3. The consent of the prospective bride and bridegroom as well as the consent of the guardian (*wali*) (Kasozi, 2004) and two witnesses are the other conditions necessary for a valid Muslim marriage.

The Muslim marriages in Uganda are conducted under the rules of the Shafi'is School of Islamic law. The Muslim marriages are normally solemnised with the help of the *Qadi* (locally spelt as khadi). However, in the absence of the *Qadi*, the Imam of the area can deputise for the Qadi. The solemnisation of a Muslim marriage in Uganda takes place in the Qadi's office or in the house of the father's bride or the guardian's house, if the bride has no father.

It is crystal clear from the Qur'anic injunctions stated here that the institution of marriage in Islam is founded on divine law. Hence, it is both a social and a religious institution. Indeed, marriage in Islam is a very important relationship, not only in people's physical life but also in their moral and spiritual life. Its effects extend, not only to the husband and wife or wives, but also to children and future generations. The Muslim marriage is the foundation of a good family, of a good society, and of a good nation. It is a sacred institution governed by sacred laws as will be seen from the following brief discussion on the foundations of Islamic legislation.

The Foundations of Islamic Legislation

To Muslims, the Qur'an, being the very word of Allah, is the authority wherefrom emanates the very conception of legality, and every legal obligation. Among the Muslims, there is no doubt that the only main lawgiver is Allah.

Every other legislating authority must base its legitimacy on revelation. The Qur'an repeatedly stresses this point. Thus it says. (*Surah* 12:40): 'The command is for none but Allah: He hath commanded that ye worship (obey) none but Him: that is the right religion (path)'. It adds (*Surah* 7:3): 'Follow (O men!) the revelation given unto you from your Lord, and follow not, as friends or protectors, other than Him'. And, although the Prophet Muhammad legislated on the basis of expediency, welfare and prosperity of society, his legitimacy was still derived from the will of God. The Qur'an (*Surah* 59:7) commands the faithful to 'take what the Messenger gives you, and refrain from what he prohibits you'.

The Prophet Muhammad legislated on the basis of the revelations and thus his role as a lawgiver was only that of a messenger. This is emphasised by the Qur'anic revelation: 'Nor does he say (aught) of (his own) desire. It is no less than inspiration sent down to him' (*Surah* 53:3 and 4.) We further read in the Qur'an: 'O Messenger!

Proclaim the (message) which hath been sent to thee from thy Lord. The Prophet Muhammad also legislated as the leader of the state for the purpose of running the affairs of the state and society. This function of legislating can be deduced from the revelation (*Surah* 48: 10) that says: 'Verily those who plight their fealty to thee [the Prophet Muhammad] plight their fealthy in truth to Allah'. This gives the Prophet Muhammad the role of a lawgiver as that of a leader.

Therefore, in Islamic legislation, the legitimacy of laws is derived solely from Allah and the Prophet Muhammad is ranked as the second main lawgiver after Allah. For this reason, the Qur'an and the *Sunna* establish two fundamental pillars on which Islamic legislation rests. The structure of the Sharia was consummated during the lifetime of the Prophet Muhammad, in the Qur'an and the *Sunna*. Thus the basic rules of Islamic law are only those prescribed in the sharia. For it should be realised that Islamic law is the epitome of the spirit, the most typical manifestation of the Islamic way of life, the kernel of Islam itself.

The most important point to note about the theoretical foundations of an Islamic legal system is that in Islam the disputes over the question of whether the foundation of a law is based on the divine authority or popular will have had separate trends. And there has not been any convergence of these trends. But in Western Europe, at the time of the Renaissance, the divine will as the foundation of government and legislation was replaced by the will of the people. And, while in an Islamic state people do elect their representatives to parliament, the very same representatives must conform to the overall principles of Islam in enacting laws, and not necessarily the will of the electorate.

Muslim Marriage under Threat

The rights to marry up to four wives, and to divorce by repudiation, are highly treasured, particularly by the Muslim men, as opposed to Muslim women, in Uganda. Forty-eight respondents, representing 68 percent, listed marrying four wives, or marrying in accordance with the Islamic law, divorce by repudiation, and inheritance in accordance with the Islamic laws, to be among the most treasured religious rights of the Muslims. Not surprisingly they bitterly criticised the Domestic Relations Bill of 1989, arguing that it infringed upon these rights.

The Domestic Relations Bill has had a long history that is well known to the interested parties and need not be discussed here. Suffice it to say here that, although the 2003 version of the Bill, which is now before parliament for debate, is the result of several revisions, nevertheless, it is still found obnoxious by the generality of the Muslim population in the country. This is hardly surprising, however.

The Qur'an bestows upon a Muslim man the right to marry up to four wives if he wishes and provided that he can treat them justly in material things as well as in affection, and the right to divorce his wife or wives by repudiation. To Muslims, who truly believe that the Qur'an is the word of God incarnate and that it is infalliable, the Muslim man's right to marry up to four wives and the right to divorce his wife or wives by repudiation, are inalienable rights which he cannot give away and which cannot be taken away from him by man-made laws. And yet this is the raison d'etre for the 2003 Domestic Relations Bill whenever it becomes law. Section 31(1) of the Bill provides, for example, that: where a man, referred to in this Act as the applicant, is a party to an Islamic or customary marriage, intends to marry a subsequent wife, he shall make an application to the District Registrar of Marriages supported by a declaration showing that he:-

1. Is economically capable of maintaining his wives and children.

2. Has made provision for a separate matrimonial home for the subsequent wife.

3. Is capable of giving the same treatment to all the wives.

The Bill also requires the applicant to obtain the consent of the first wife that she has no objection to polygamy. Where the District Registrar is satisfied that the applicant has complied with all the conditions set out in subsection (1) and, that in addition, he has obtained the consent of his first wife to polygamy, he shall approve the application for the subsequent marriage to take place under this Act, otherwise he shall reject the application!

Section 31(1) of the Domestic Relations Bill is an encroachment upon a man's right to marry up to four wives unhindered. Its object is to drastically restrict the practice of polygamy among the Muslim population in the country. Yet, from the Muslim's point of view, man-made laws cannot have precedence over God's laws, i.e. Qur'anic injunctions. Thus Muslims are bound to regard the conditions laid down in the Domestic Relations Bill pertaining to marriage as direct interference with their freedom of worship.

The Qur'an, as was seen in Chapter 4, also bestows upon a Muslim man the right to divorce his wife, or wives, by repudiation. But the Domestic Relations Bill seeks to subvert this right. Section 79 of the Bill provides, for example (see Kasozi, 2004), that: 'a spouse shall not petition for divorce before the expiry of two years from the date of the marriage which is sought to be dissolved'. Certainly, if this provision were to become law, it would negate the Muslim man's God-given right to divorce his wife or wives by repudiation. Furthermore, this would not go down well with the Muslim population who, rightly, would regard it as a serious infringement upon their religious rights. They are also likely to regard it as null and void since, from their perception of life, God-given laws take precedence over man-made ones.

As we noted earlier, for a Muslim marriage to be valid, it requires a dower or gift (*mahr*) for the wife. The *mahr*, as will be seen from *Surah*, 4:4 quoted above, is obligatory on every man who wishes to solemnise a Muslim marriage. It is a mandatory marriage gift which is given by the bridegroom to his bride at the time of their marriage. The Qur'an lays great emphasis on the personal nature of the *mahr* so that it would be wrong to equate it with bride-price. But, despite the fact that the law commanding men to give their brides dower is God-given and that the dower is socially innocuous, it is not to be spared by the Domestic Relations Bill if ever it is enacted into law. Section 20(1) of the Bill provides, for instance (Kasozi, 2004), that marriage gifts shall not be an essential requirement for any marriage under this Act. This provision, like the others cited previously, is in direct contravention of the God-given legislation on Muslim marriage.

It is small wonder, then, that the Muslim population in the country regard the Domestic Relations Bill with alarm and bewilderment. Indeed the Bill is punctuated by articles which are in direct contravention of the Qur'anic injunctions and other tenets of Islam. Kasozi (Kasozi, 2004) outlines some of these articles. This has, provoked some of the Muslim leaders into openly criticising the provisions of the Domestic Relations Bill as 'part of a wider anti-Islam agenda' (Kasozi, 2004). Indeed, many Muslim leaders who were not included in our sample have also vociferously criticised the Domestic Relations Bill for its infringement upon the religious rights of Muslims. For example, on 18 January 1998, the former Chairman of the Electoral Commission, Hajj Aziz K. Kasujja, told a Ramadhan Annual Convention which was held at the Islamic University in Uganda, Mbale, that the Domestic Relations Bill was an attempt to Christianise Muslims by not allowing them to marry in accordance with the Qur'an (*The Monitor*, 19 Jan. 1989). For his part, the Chairman of the Uganda Muslim Youth Assembly (UMYA), Dr Abasi Kiyimba, told a seminar held at Sheraton Hotel, Kampala, on 9 January 1998, that the Domestic Relations Bill, which requires that, in order to marry a second wife, a man should obtain the consent of his first wife, was a breach of the sharia which leaves the choice of either marrying one or four wives to the individual. (*The Monitor*, 11 Jan. 1998). He further cautioned the audience that the proposed bill was also in violation of Articles 7 and 21 of the 1995 Ugandan constitution which guarantees freedom of worship.

That Article 31(1) of the Domestic Relations Bill requires a man with the intention of marrying a second wife to apply to the District Registrar of Marriages for permission to do so is a negation of the sharia. This is because it aims at depriving a Muslim man of his freedom of worship, since Islam takes marriage as a form of worship. Thus many respondents (73 per cent) objected to Article 9 of the Domestic Relations Bill requiring licensing of places of marriage on the grounds that this is outright interference with the freedom of worship and that it imposes unnecessary hardships on couples intending to marry. In fact, in the opinion of the Chairman of the UMYA (*The Monitor*, 23 March 1999), 'the effect of the Domestic Relations Bill will be to weaken the institution of marriage and organised society as we know it in Islam.' The opponents of the Domestic Relations Bill secured vital support from *The Monitor*, which wrote in its editorial of 18 January 1998 thus: 'Muslims are right to view this law as an insult and as an attempt by the powers that be, to impose a secular concept of marriage on them.' The quest for uniformity in social laws in a multi-religious society, like that of Uganda, is bound to result in injustices to minority groups. In fact, Muslims truly feel that they are treated as third-class citizens because of being a minority.

Of course, the structure of Islamic societies has been modified through the ages in response to changes in time and place. But always care has been taken to ensure that the reforms and changes effected conform to the sharia. Thus it is a requirement that proposed modifications to Islamic practices should be scrutinised by the *ulama* (learned men; particularly those learned in the Muslim sciences of the traditions and the sacred law) for purposes of giving a legal opinion as to whether or not the proposed reforms conform to the sharia. The Egyptian government, for example, referred the Family Status bill, which allows Egyptian women to divorce their husbands on grounds of incompatibility within three months, if they return their dowry and waive their right to alimony, to al-Azhar University in Cairo for a legal opinion as regards the Bill's conformity to the sharia, before tabling it in parliament for debate on 16 January 2000. Al-Azhar University has the reputation of being the custodian of Islamic values in Egypt. With the green light from the authorities of al-Azhar University, the bill was finally enacted into law on 27 January 2000. Until the enactment of this law, Egyptian women wishing to divorce their husbands, had to face many years of court action. However, Egyptian men will still divorce their wives by repudiation, i.e. by simply saying 'I divorce you' in accordance with the sharia.

But, as the Mufti of Uganda, Sheikh Shaban R. Mubajje (*The Sunday Vision*, Nov. 3, 2002:29) recently stated, marriage in Islam is not a temporary bond as the ardent proponents of the Domestic Relations Bill would have us believe. It is meant for life, although, if it fails completely, divorce is permissible. And, contrary to Dr Specioza Kazibwe's fantastic claim (Ibid.) that 'Islam beats all other religions in granting immediate divorce to a disgruntled married couple', the sharia frowns on instant divorce, as will be seen from the procedures laid down for effecting a divorce under the sharia. (These procedures were discussed in Chapter 4.)

The example cited here is not peculiar to Egypt, however. In fact, it is a common practice among states which profess to enforce the sharia, e.g. Sudan, Iran and Pakistan, to refer controversial legislation to a council of the *ulama* for legal opinion on its conformity to the sharia. It was a serious omission, therefore, for the Uganda Law Reform Commission, not to have referred the Domestic Relations Bill to the UMSC for legal opinion on its compatibility with the sharia before handing it over to the government. We need to take cognizance of the fact that the sharia always remains valid, whether or not it is recognised by the state. Hence a law which openly contravenes the sharia is not likely to command legitimacy among the Muslim population. And, as such, it will be openly flouted by those who regard it as illegitimate. In fact, recently (2004) Imam Iddi Kasozi, the Vice-Chairman, Uganda Muslim Youth Assembly, told the 17th Annual Ramadhan Convention which was held at the IUIU, Mbale, in October 2004 (Kasozi, 2004), that the Domestic Relations Bill was authored in bad faith and that Muslims would have nothing to do with it if ever it became law. He then exhorted the proponents of the bill to leave Muslims alone to manage their family affairs in accordance with Islamic social laws.

It is very curious indeed that we should be contemplating to replace the Islamic personal law which so far has proved to be successful, with a Westernised secularist family law par excellence that seems to have been transplanted from Europe's most secular and most liberal states – Denmark, Sweden and Norway – where similar laws have led to divorce rates of over 60 percent in the past three decades! It should also be realised that Uganda, as a member state of the Organisation of Islamic Conference, is under treaty obligations to assist the Muslim minority in our midst to preserve its religion and to live in accordance with its principles and teachings. Undoubtedly, a perfidious law such as the Domestic Relations Bill, that infringes upon a man's right to marry up to four wives, and to divorce by repudiation; that encroaches upon a wife's right to receive the *mahr* from her husband; that revokes a father's right to consent to his daughter's marriage; that promotes cohabitation and perhaps gay marriages; that sanctions marriage between dying partners; that encroaches upon the husband's right to decide on the inheritance of the matrimonial property; in utter disregard and contempt of the Islamic law and Islamic principles and teachings, does not augur well for the survival of the institution of Muslim marriage and family as we know them today. Nor is it conducive to a harmonious environment in which the Muslim population can practise their religion unperturbed. Nor does it augur well for the social stability of Ugandan society.

6

From Timidity to Self-assertiveness

The Islamic Resurgence

While Asians became increasingly assertive as a result of economic development (see Harrison and Huntington, 2000:244-266), Muslims in massive numbers were simultaneously turning towards Islam as a source of identity, meaning, stability, legitimacy, development, power, and a hope, hope epitomised in the slogan 'Islam is the solution'. This Islamic Resurgence in its extent and profundity is the latest phase in the adjustment of Islamic civilisation to the West, an effort to find the solution not in Western ideologies but in Islam. It embodies acceptance of modernity, rejection of Western culture, and recommitment to Islam as the guide to life in the modern world.

The Islamic Resurgence is the effort by Muslims to achieve modernisation without being Westernised. It is a broad intellectual, cultural, social, and political movement prevalent throughout the Islamic world. Thus Islamic fundamentalism is only one component in the much more extensive revival of Islamic ideas, practices, and rhetoric and the redediction to Islam by Muslim populations. The Resurgence is mainstream not extremist, pervasive not isolated. It has affected Muslims in every country and most aspects of society and politics in most Muslim countries.

The indices of an Islamic awakening in personal life are many: increased attention to religious observances, proliferation of religious programming and publications, more emphasis on Islamic dress and values; and the revitalisation of Sufism (mysticism). This broader-based renewal (Esposito, 1992:12) has also been accompanied by

Islam's reassertion in public life: an increase in Islamically oriented governments, and educational institutions. Both governments and opposition movements have turned to Islam to enhance their authority and muster popular support.

The Islamic Resurgence can also be seen (Dessouki, 1982:9-13) as involving efforts to re-institute Islamic law in place of Western law, the increased use of religious language and symbolism, expansion of Islamic education – manifested in the Islamisation of the curricula in regular state schools –, increased adherence to Islamic codes of social behaviour, and increased participation in religious observances and expanding efforts to develop international solidarity among Islamic states and societies.

In its political manifestations, the Islamic Resurgence bears a resemblance to Marxism, with scriptural texts, a vision of the perfect society, commitment to fundamental change, rejection of powers that be and the nation state, and doctrinal diversity ranging from moderate reformist to violent revolutionary. Like the Protestant Reformation before it, the Islamic Resurgence is a reaction to the stagnation and corruption of existing institutions. The central spirit of the Islamic Resurgence is fundamental reform. Thus Dr Hassan al-Turabi (al-Turabi, 1992:52) asserts, 'this awakening is comprehensive – it is not just about individual piety; it is not just intellectual and cultural, nor is it just political. It is all of these, a comprehensive reconstruction of society from top to bottom'.

The Islamic Resurgence has touched almost every Muslim society. Beginning in the 1970s, Islamic symbols, beliefs, practices, institutions, policies, and organisations won increasing commitment and support throughout the Muslim world. Intellectual and political leaders, whether they favoured Islamisation or not, could neither ignore it nor avoid adapting to it in one way or another. Thus, it is on record (Huntington, 1996:111) that in 1995 every country with a predominantly Muslim population, except Iran, was more Islamic and Islamist culturally, socially, and politically than it was fifteen years earlier.

The political manifestations of the Resurgence have been less pervasive than its social and cultural manifestations, but they still are the single most important political development in Muslim societies in the last quarter of the twentieth century. The extent and makeup of the political support for Islamist movements has varied from country to country. Yet certain broad tendencies exist. By and large those movements do not get much support from rural elites, peasants, and the elderly. Like fundamentalists in other religions, Islamists are overwhelmingly participants in and products of the process of modernisation. They are mobile and modern-oriented younger people drawn in large part from three groups: students and intellectuals, urban middle-class people, and recent migrants to the cities and towns. The mass of revolutionary Islam is a product of modern society: the new urban arrivals, and the millions of peasants who have tripled the populations of the great Muslim-metropolises to whom Islam offers a dignified identity.

During the 1970s and 1980s a wave of democratisation swept across the world, encompassing several dozen countries. This wave had an impact on Muslim societies, but it was a limited one. While democratic movements were gaining strength and coming to power in southern Europe, Latin America, the East Asian periphery, Central Europe and sub-Saharan Africa, Islamist movements were simultaneously gaining strength in Muslim countries. Islamism was the functional substitute for the democratic opposition to authoritarianism in Christian societies, and it was in large part the product of similar causes: social mobilisation, loss of performance legitimacy by authoritarian regimes, and a changing international environment, including oil price increases, which in the Muslim world encouraged Islamist rather than democratic trends.

Thus in the 1980s and 1990s Islamist movements dominated and often monopolised the opposition to governments in Muslim countries. Their strength was in part a function of the weakness of alternative sources of opposition. Leftist and communist movements had been discredited and then seriously undermined by the collapse of the Soviet Union and international communism. Liberal, democratic opposition groups had existed in most Muslim societies but were usually confined to limited numbers of intellectuals and others with Western roots or connections. The general failure of liberal democracy to take hold in Muslim societies is a continuing and repeated phenomenon for an entire century beginning in the late 1880s. This failure has its source at least in part in the incompatibility of Islamic culture and society with Western liberal concepts.

The Islamic Resurgence is both a product of and an effort to come to grips with modernisation. Its underlying causes (Huntington, 1996:16) are those generally responsible for indigenisation trends in non-Western societies: urbanisation, social mobilisation, higher levels of literacy and education, intensified communication and media consumption, and expanded interaction with Western and other cultures. These developments undermine traditional villages and clan ties and create alienation and an identity crisis. Islamist symbols, commitments, and beliefs meet these psychological needs. And Islamist welfare organisations meet the economic needs of Muslims caught in the process of modernisation. Muslims feel the need to return to Islamic ideas, practices, and institutions which would then provide the compass and the motor of modernisation.

The Islamic revival was also a product of the West's declining power and prestige. The Resurgence was stimulated and fuelled by the oil boom of the 1970s, which greatly increased the wealth and power of many Muslim nations and enabled them to reverse the relations of domination and subordination that had existed with the West. The Saudi, Libyan, and other governments used their oil riches to stimulate and finance the Muslim revival, and Muslim wealth led Muslims to swing from fascination with Western culture to deep involvement in their own and willingness to assert the place and importance of Islam in non-Islamic societies.

Futile Attempts at Forming an Islamic Political Party

The following discussion focuses on Ugandan Muslims' recently found vigour and pertinacity in clamouring for the observance of the religio-political rights of Muslims. This development is quite amazing, realising that, as late as the 1960s, it was very rare for Muslims to openly use their Muslim names, particularly if they attended mission schools, or if they were candidates seeking employment in government departments, out of the fear that they would be victimised on the basis of their faith. This fear was not totally unfounded, however. It is common knowledge that the British colonial administration in Uganda (1900 – 1962) discriminated against Muslims in the country, particularly in the enrolment of the clientele of post-primary education institutions and in the recruitment of staff for the government and its agencies. This was not peculiar to the Muslim population in Uganda, however. Muslims in other British territories in Africa, with the notable exception of Sudan, suffered the same fate as their co-religionists in Uganda. (On the British attitude towards Muslims in West Africa see, e.g., Hiskett, 1984:276-309.) Generally speaking, British administrators in Africa held the view that Islam was anti-British rule and that, if African Muslims acquired a knowledge of the English language through schooling, they would become easy prey to the 'nationalist demagogues' that were expected to emerge from Western-educated natives.

Therefore, the policy of the British administrations in territories with Muslim populations was to frustrate their efforts to acquire education and to deny them government salaried employment which, in the colonial economy, was the only form of lucrative employment. Of course, without this kind of employment Western-educated Muslims were most unlikely to gain positions of social influence in society or to earn enough money to educate their children. However, for special considerations, British administrators in Sudan adopted a more accommodating approach to the Muslim question. They deemed it politically judicious to educate Arab Sudanese and to make them partners in the running of their country in order to raise their national consciousness as a counter force to Egyptian nationalism which posed a serious challenge to British rule in Sudan.

Thus the discrimination suffered by the Muslim population in Uganda at the hands of the British colonial rulers had its origins in the grand plan of the British government to ward off a possible revolt in Africa by Western-educated, English-speaking Muslims. From the British point of view these people were more likely to be disgruntled at British rule and to work for its overthrow than their unschooled kinsmen.

Not surprisingly, up till the 1970s, Muslims in Uganda believed, rightly or wrongly, that they were subjected to relentless discrimination by state authorities on the basis of their religion. They seemed to acquiesce in their status of 'third-class citizens' with little fury, however.

Today, Uganda's Muslim population is one of the boldest and most vocal groups in demanding the protection of minority rights, i.e., religio-political rights of Muslims, in the country. Thanks to Idi Amin's regime (1971-79) which, through its pro-Islam policies such as the promotion of Islamic education, making Friday a non-working day for public employees, taking Uganda into the OIC, and broadcasting the news in Arabic – the language of Islam – by Radio Uganda, helped to instil in the Muslim population a high sense of group identity as well as giving them the much-needed sense of self-confidence. And, if nothing else, the overthrow of Idi Amin's regime in 1979, and the subsequent restoration of Christian rulers, galvanised the Muslim population into fighting tooth and nail to hold onto the socio-political and economic gains which they had made under Idi Amin's rule. Furthermore, Muslims wanted to make sure that Islam was not once again relegated to obscurity by Amin's successors as was the case before Amin's era. Of course, as shown above, the assertiveness of the Muslim population in Uganda was, and still is, fuelled by the world-wide Islamic Resurgence. It is against this background that Ugandan Muslims' demand for the observance of the rights of Muslims in Uganda can be understood and appreciated.

In the light of what has been said so far, we can conjecture that before Idi Amin's rule and perhaps during Amin's rule itself (1971-

78) Muslims in Uganda experienced a crisis of identity. However, for the reasons discussed below, in the post-Amin era, they were able to develop a positive sense of identity. There were crucial factors, both internal and external, which significantly contributed to the rise of Islamic consciousness and to a high sense of commitment to the observance of the Qur'anic injunctions among the Muslim population in Uganda. The most important internal factor responsible for raising Islamic consciousness among Uganda's Muslims was the alleged or real marginalisation and persecution of Muslims as a group or as individuals, particularly immediately after the overthrow of Amin's regime in April 1979.

In some parts of the country, the overthrow of Amin's regime was followed by spontaneous persecution of Muslims or wanton revenge attacks against them for Amin's regime's atrocities. It was in this environment that the Muslim leaders who stayed in the country tried to reorganise the Muslim community under the leadership of Prince Badru Kakungulu. They decided (Kanyeihamba, 1988: 17) to revamp the UMSC administration under the leadership of Kassim Mulumba with Sheikh Ali Kivumbi and Sheikh Muhammad Semakula as his deputies. Their chief aim was to prepare themselves to resist further persecution and marginalisation by the state bureaucracies. Indeed, it is in the crucible of political crisis and rebellion that people become more conscious of their own latent aspirations and understanding of the world, even as they redefine or perhaps transform them. The chaos that followed the overthrow of Idi Amin's regime created such an opportunity for the Muslim population in the country. A shared sense of Islamic identification and grievance served as a bridge, uniting the loyalties of Muslims of different sects. The Muslim leaders of the day knew, or ought to have known, that sustainable unity of the Muslims in Uganda could only be achieved if it were backed by an Islamic-based ideology which could then be used to mobilise the Muslim masses. This ideology was to be found in a revival, or a resurgence; but it is also a return to the foundations of Islam; what outsiders call Islamic fundamentalism. Thus, the past two decades have seen a tremendous increase in Islamic consciousness among Uganda's Muslims and a huge growth in Islamic fundamentalism. Of course, as it has been observed (Kayunga, 1993:39-41), the tempo of the increase in Islamic consciousness among Uganda's Muslims and the growth of Islamic fundamentalism has been influenced, and continues to be influenced, by external factors.

The Iranian revolution of 1978, for example, gave Muslims the world over, including those in Uganda, a lot of hope and encouragement in their struggle against secularism and Western cultural domination. Above all, Ugandan youths who studied in Islamic countries, particularly Pakistan, during the 1980s and 1990s, were usually exposed to radical trends within the Islamic faith and, on their return home, took it upon themselves to reform the Islamic practices in the country, thus arousing Islamic consciousness among the faithful, particularly the young generation. It is hardly surprising, therefore (Kayunga, 1993:39-40), that the founding members of the Tabliq Youths Movement, were all graduates of Pakistani colleges and universities. The Tabliq Youths Movement is an Islamic religio-social organisation that exhorts its members and Muslims in general to strictly observe Islamic practices and to make these practices part of their daily life.

The other external factor which has greatly contributed to the increase of Islamic consciousness among Uganda's Muslims, thus laying the ground for the growth of radical Islam in Uganda, is the proliferation of Muslim NGOs. Since the inception of the NRM government in 1986, the Muslim NGOs – most of which are based in foreign Islamic states and are foreign funded, e.g. the Islamic African Relief Agency, the International Islamic Charitable Foundation, the Munadhamat al-Dawa al-Islamiya; the African Muslim Agency, the International Islamic Call Society, and the Muslim World League – have played a critical role in the Islamic revival in Uganda in various ways. They construct schools, medical centres, and mosques, which not only are important in the propagation of Islam but also boost the self-confidence of the Muslim population in the country. This in itself is gradually creating over-confidence among the Muslim radicals and this has emboldened them enough to demand an Islamic state. Also, the rise of Islamic consciousness and a high sense of commitment to the observance of the Qur'anic injunctions among the Muslim population in Uganda was greatly influenced by the world-wide Islamic Resurgence for the reasons stated earlier.

On closer observation, the postulates of the radical Islamists reveal mere prophecies, advice, threats and general desiderata with a programme that has little consistency. Thus radical Islamic fundamentalism fails to solve factual problems, offering mostly regressive attempts at solutions precisely because its orientation is mythical, but otherwise restorative, and hardly utopian. It thus promotes a revolutionary society. In fact, Islamists usually promise a righteous society, here and now, through the catharsis, i.e. a transformation from corruption to purity, and from *jahiliya* to Islam. However, since the 1980s one can detect a change in the Islamist discourse. This is particularly true in postmodern times where political Islam has failed, because Islamist promises were not realised owing to the fact that they were often unrealistic and utopian. And, parallel to this failure, new alternatives have emerged, reflecting the interaction of different social realities and cultural identities in a pluralising society in which Islamists have also started increasingly to use ideas of mythical re-establishments to mark out their social and political territories and to enlarge them, albeit within the existing nation-states.

In this phase of post-Islamism, the Islamists' own position is constantly re-negotiated vis-à-vis the government, external patrons, other Islamist groups, and the masses or the target audiences. This involves competition and contest over interpretation of symbols and control of institutions; because symbols are an integral part of Muslim politics (Malick, http://www.isim). They express the values and are constitutive of a political community. Hence there is a constant struggle concerning people's imagination and, following that, about the objective chances and resources in a free market, thus opening the way for the formation of a political party with an Islamic platform to compete for state power. These developments were reinforced by the electoral success of the Islamic Salvation Front (FIS) in the 1991/92 Algerian national elections which the Algerian government shamefully cancelled when it saw that the FIS was heading for clear victory. The Islamic Salvation Front's short-lived electoral success persuaded Islamist groups, particularly those in Africa, to accept the efficacy of the 'ballot box' as a dependable means of attaining state power.

It is against this background that attempts to form the Uganda Islamic Revolutionary Party (UIRP) can be appreciated. Islam by nature is not a hierarchical religion, thus enabling self-appointed 'leaders' to speak on behalf of the Muslim community in Uganda. Thus, when on 28 April 1993 Mr Idris Muwonge, together with 30 members of the Tabliq Youths Movement, announced the formation of the UIRP, their right to act and speak on behalf of the Muslim population in such an important matter as forming a political party could not be dismissed as wishful thinking. This was in spite of the fact that in some Muslim circles Mr Muwonge, who declared himself the Chairman of the UIRP, is not highly regarded. The formation of the UIRP was in conformity with the trend in most parts of the Muslim world where, since the 1980s, forward-looking Muslims have formed Islamic-based political parties to contest for state power through elections within a liberal democratic setting. The formation of the Islamic Party of Kenya (IPK) in February 1992 gave added impetus to the formation of the UIRP.

Moreover, historically (Karugire, 1980:148-68), Uganda has had religious-political parties like the Catholic sponsored DP and the largely Protestant UPC since the formation of national parties in the late 1950s and early 1960s. Hence up till 1993 Muslims were the only major religious group in Uganda without a political party of its own. Under these circumstances Muslims, or a majority of them at any rate, aligned themselves with one of the existing parties that seemed to have better prospects of winning state power at an election. But with the substantial increase in the number of the Muslim elites during the past three decades, the necessity for the

Muslim population to continue to swing from one political party to another has decreased, thus increasing the need for Muslims to form their own political party.

Above all, the political parties with which the Muslims have so far aligned themselves at different times, i.e. the UPC in the 1960s, the DP in the 1980s, and presently the NRM, have all woefully failed to protect and foster the rights of Muslims in the country and instead have been accused, among other things, of deliberately marginalising the Muslim elites, especially in the procurement of government posts. Therefore, the main objectives of the UIRP (Kayunga, 1993:75), according to Muwonge, 'is to struggle for the Muslim rights'. The other aims of the UIRP include: encouraging Muslims to actively participate in the political, social, and economic affairs of Uganda; establishing a government based on Islamic principles; and implementing the sharia. Muwonge threatened that, if the government refused to register his party, it would operate clandestinely. To him, and those like him in the Tabliq Youths Movement, the government's refusal to register the UIRP would mean that Muslims in Uganda were denied their political rights since the Catholics and Protestants have their own respective political parties.

Muwonge's fears that the NRM government might not register the UIRP have since come true. This is hardly surprising, however. It was most unlikely that the NRM government, which on many occasions has publicly denounced sectarianism and religious-political parties as inappropriate for a democratic Uganda, would register an Islamic party like the UIRP. Nor is it likely to be registered in the foreseeable future now that Parliament has enacted a law, 'The Political Parties and Organisations Act, 2002' (Uganda Government, 2002:7-12), to outlaw the formation of sectarian and religious-political parties altogether. It is not clear, however, to what extent the UIRP is carrying out its threat to operate underground and to use Islam as an ideology to mobilise the Muslim masses to demand their political rights. But the apparent lack of enthusiasm for the UIRP among the Muslim population, particularly the older generation who incidentally still dominate the leadership of the UMSC, is bound to make this task an arduous one.

That the older generation of Muslims were not fiercely loyal to the UIRP is not surprising, however. As we noted in the discussion on the Islamic Resurgence, Islamists everywhere are mobile and modern-oriented younger people drawn in large part from among students and intellectuals, urban middle-class people, and recent migrants to the cities and towns. Therefore, it would be illusionary to regard the lack of enthusiasm among the older generation of Muslims in Uganda for the formation of an Islamic party as a sign of its unpopularity generally.

Opposition to Political Parties

That the Movement government tenaciously opposed the formation of the UIRP is hardly surprising. The Movement's political philosophy rests on the premise that Uganda's political culture is not particularly conducive to a Western-style democratic system built around political parties and periodic elections contested by candidates sponsored by political parties. The goals of the Movement are to exclusively educate the population generally and politically with a view to promote national integration and to build a national civic identity or culture.

The top leadership of the Movement accepts participation but not the necessity to organise it. Theirs is a populistic, Rousseauian belief in direct democracy. They deny the need for any intervening structure between the people and its political leaders. They favour a 'partyless democracy'. They view political parties as an obstacle to the expression of the general will of the people and see no relevance of parties to political modernisation. The leadership of the Movement, like other opponents of parties in modernising societies, make four principal charges against political parties[1]:

1. Parties promote corruption and administrative inefficiency.[2]

2. They split society against itself and promote conflict.[3]

3. They encourage political instability and political weakness.[4]
4. They lay the state open to influence from and penetration by external powers.

The arguments against parties are, in fact, less arguments against parties than they are arguments against weak parties. Corruption, division, instability, and susceptibility to outside influence all characterise weak party systems rather than strong ones. They are, indeed, features of weak political systems generally, which lack stable and effective institutions of rule.

Of course, there is some truth in the charges levelled against political parties. In the 1960s and 1970s Westernised and pro-Western governments in developing countries were threatened by coups d'etat and revolution; in the 1980s, 1990s and currently, they are increasingly in danger of being ousted by elections. Democratisation conflicts with Westernisation and democracy are inherently a parochialising, not a cosmopolitanising, process. Politicians in non-Western societies do not win elections by demonstrating how Western they are. Electoral competition instead stimulates them to fashion what they believe will be the most popular appeals, and those are usually ethnic, nationalist, and religious in character. The result is, at least in Muslim countries, popular mobilisation against Western-educated and western-oriented elites. Islamic fundamentalist groups have done well in the few elections that have occurred in Muslim countries and would have come to national power in Algeria if the military had not cancelled the 1992 elections. In India (Funabashi, 1992:24) competition for electoral support has arguably encouraged communal appeals and communal violence.

True enough, parties may also furnish incentives to corruption, but the development of a strong political party substitutes an institutionalised public interest for fragmented private ones. In their early stages of development, political parties appear as factions and seemingly exacerbate conflict and disunity, but as they develop strength parties become the buckle which binds one social force to another and which creates a basis for loyalty and identity transcending mere parochial groupings. Similarly, by regularising the procedures for leadership succession and for the assimilation of new groups into the political system, parties provide the basis for stability and orderly change rather than for instability. The evils attributed to parties are, in reality, the attributes of a disorganised and fragmented politics of clique and faction which prevails when political parties are non-existent or still very weak. Their cure lies in political organisation; and in a modernising state political organisation means party organization.

Of course, such party organisation does not rule out the formation of either religious parties or tribal ones, since, as we have noted, in their early stages of development, political parties appear as factions to champion the interests of parochial groupings. A party is strong to the extent that it has institutionalised mass support. Its strength reflects the scope of that support and the level of institutionalisation. But all this takes time to develop. And, in a society with fluid open-ended fabrics like ours, it is unrealistic to expect political parties to have institutionalised mass support at their inception. Surely, in a democracy any group of people who feel that they are being marginalised by the government of the day should be able to exercise their constitutional right of association and form their own political party to champion their interests without being made to meet formidable requirements such as having mass support. Otherwise, democracy will remain elusive.

Moreover, in today's era of the Islamic Resurgence, Muslims in Uganda, like their counterparts elsewhere, are called upon to find solutions to the multiplicity of societal problems that currently face the country, not in Western ideologies but in Islam. And, unless they have their own political party and are able to compete for state power, their efforts to make Islam the panacea of all Uganda's problems will not receive the widespread publicity and support that it deserves. Muslims in the existing political organisations – the Movement, the DP, and UPC – all of which are Western-oriented, will not be allowed to advocate an Islamic platform, since such a move would be regarded as sectarian.

And, since the existing parties adhere to the christo-ideology and culture that is inherently deleterious to Islam and Islamic civilisation, and since the Muslim population has special socio-economic and religio-political needs that can only be catered for by a party with an Islamic platform, it is imperative that they should have their own political party to articulate these needs. Otherwise, they are bound to feel that they are deliberately marginalised by today's rulers regardless of whether or not some members of the Muslim community hold top positions in the government of the day.

It is small wonder, then, that in 1987 (Quality, 1987:34-35), Sheikh Abubakar M. Gumi, a King Faisal laureate, enunciated that: 'The two-party system of government [in his country, Nigeria] will not be South against North but Islam against Christianity. [For]', as he put it, 'once you are a good Moslem, you cannot vote for or accept a non-Moslem to be your leader.' He further contended that Muslims would not allow a Christian to be leader of a political party 'if there are Moslems in that party.' This leaves Muslims with no option but to have their own political party if, in Sheikh Gumi's opinion (Quality, 1987:37), they are to avoid the possibility of compromising Islam as well as to carry out their most noble duty which is 'to try to convert Christians and other non-Moslems as much as possible [through enlightenment] until the other religions become [innocuous minorities].'

It can be surmised from what has been said about political parties so far that the vigorous opposition mounted by the top leadership of the Movement against the formation of the UIRP, which culminated in the enactment of the Political Parties and Organisations Act (2002), is nothing less than a camouflage for the Movement's long-standing anti-party stance rather than represenitng its overt opposition to sectarian parties per se. It is an effort on the part of the Movement leaders to reduce the amount of political power and to restrict both political participation and the organisations associated with that participation. This anti-party attitude is not peculiar to the Movement, however. Huntington (Huntington, 1968:403) reminds us, for example, that 'traditional polities do not have political parties; modernising polities [like Uganda] need them but often do not want them.'

And, although President Yoweri K. Museveni and other top leaders of the NRM party grudgingly campaigned for a 'yes' vote in the referendum, which was held on 28 July 2005, to decide whether or not Uganda should retain the 'Movement political system', i.e. the no-party system, or adopt a multiparty political system, there is little doubt that they remain totally unconvinced of the relevance of parties to political modernisation in Uganda today. The question which voters were asked to answer in the referendum ran like this: 'Do you agree to open up the political space to allow those who wish to join different organisations/parties to do so to compete for political power?' The results of the referendum showed that the overwhelming majority (92.5%) of those who cared to vote (47%) cast their vote for 'yes', thus opening the way for a return to multiparty politics after two decades of no-party rule. However, it remains to be seen whether the NRM leaders who continue to vigorously support the Movement's political philosophy which, as previously stated, rests on the premise that Uganda's political culture is not particularly conducive to a Western-style democratic system built around parties and periodic elections contested by candidates sponsored by parties, will in future allow political parties to operate freely without hindrance. Indeed, the constitutional amendments which Parliament has so far passed purportedly to facilitate political transition from the 'Movement system' to multiparty system – curiously enough these constitutional amendments were drafted before the 28 July referendum was held! – do not attenuate the powers of the 'Movement' political organs in anyway or sever their connections with the state.

However, in this era of the Islamic Resurgence (see Antoun and Hegland, 1987), the UIRP's failure to secure registration as a political party can only be regarded as a temporary setback and not the end of the Muslims' project to form their own political party. The Muslim population can no longer stand idly by and wring their hands in anguish while Islam is debased by Westernised modernisation, which seems to enjoy enthusiastic support among the Christian population in the country. It will be recalled that the Islamic Resurgence is both a product of and an effort to come to grips with modernisation. However, this noble goal cannot be realised unless the country has a political party with an Islamic platform and dedicated to catering for Muslims' special needs and interests. Yet, from the nature of Uganda's religious structure and make-up, no party, other than a Muslim one, can genuinely advance an Islamic platform.

Therefore, the sooner the top leadership of the Movement drops its opposition to the formation of religious parties and grants Muslims their wish to form their own political party, the better for our country. And, if one may ask: Is there a political organisation or party in today's Uganda that can be exonerated from accusations of sectarianism? We ought to be reminded too that sectarianism is a feature of young political parties everywhere. Moreover, a society which develops reasonably well-organised political parties while the level of political participation is still relatively low, as is the case in Uganda today, is likely to have a less destabilising expansion of political participation than a society where parties are organised later in the process of political modernisation. Thus, today's rulers of Uganda would be well advised to desist from implementing policies which have great potential to radicalise Islam, or else the country will be made to pay dearly in future for the missed opportunity.

Contestation over Muslim Voters' Votes in Future National Elections

For the time being at least, today's Muslim leaders regard the NRM government as better positioned to protect the Muslims' political interests than a small and fragile Islamic party. This partly explains why in the previous national presidential and parliamentary elections in 1996 and 2001 Muslim voters voted for non-Muslim candidates in many cases at the expense of Muslim candidates. But, there are already indications that the 'new breed' of Muslim leaders, particularly those with a fundamentalist orientation, are not likely to acquiesce in the status quo much longer with or without an Islamic political party. They might throw in their lot with any political party headed by a fellow Muslim, even if it is not a self-confessed Islamic party, since such a party would have greater potential to protect and foster the interests of Muslims than parties headed by non-Muslims, no matter how well-intentioned they might be.

In the run-up to the 1996 presidential and parliamentary elections, for example, some Muslim leaders made attempts to control Muslim voters in order to select for them the candidates for whom to vote. The sponsors of this scheme argued, for instance, that Muslims had been taken for a ride by Christian politicians for a long time, and that it was now time for them to fight back, by supporting candidates with Islamic credentials. For example, in August 1995 Mr Hussein Kyanjo of the Tabliq sect badgered a congregation at Nakasero Mosque (*The Shariat*, 8-14 August 1995: 2) 'not to vote for Museveni because he was not bothered to cater for their interests.' Indeed, with increased Islamic consciousness and awareness of their religio-political rights, the Muslim population will increasingly become less disposed to vote for Christian candidates in future national elections, thus attracting special attention from Muslim candidates seeking public office. This was well demonstrated in the 2001 presidential and parliamentary elections. For example, on 23 May 2000, Mr Muhammad Kibirige Mayanja, the President of the Justice Forum, who contested the 2001 presidential elections (*The New Vision*, 24 May 2000:5), urged Muslim women during their annual *da'awa* competition at Bilali-Kakiri to vote for him in those elections 'so that Muslims can break the Christian monopoly of state power.' Mr Mayanja further told his audience that the 2001 elections would present the most opportune moment for Muslims to 'fight for the front seats,' i.e. ministerial posts. He then warned thus: 'Time is gone for us [Muslims] to sit down and watch Christians move on.'

Mr Mayanja's utterances here would seem to suggest that he, and perhaps many other young Muslim leaders, strongly believe that Uganda's Muslims are now sufficiently conscious of their rights not to wish to jeopardise them by voting for candidates of a party of non-Islamic platform. And, even if Mr Mayanja's optimism was premature - he lost the elections to president Yoweri K. Museveni - the truth of the matter is that Uganda's Muslims today are more conscious of their religio-political rights than they were at the time the NRM captured state power in 1986, and they are more determined than ever before to strive for the realisation of these rights.

Foreign Involvement in the Clamour for the Rights of Muslims

In the foregoing discussion we alluded to foreign influence in the rise of Islamic consciousness among Uganda's Muslims as well as enhancing their awareness of the religio-political rights of Muslims. Of course, these two phenomena are essential for the success of the struggle for the enforcement of the religio-political rights of Muslims in Uganda. It is a truism, for example, that the operations of the foreign-based Muslim NGOs in Uganda have boosted the self-confidence of the Muslim population in the country. This in turn has led to a rise in the degree of commitment to Islam. It can be conjectured (Kayunga, 1993:41) that it is this increased commitment to Islam and Islamic practices which has given 'rise to militant Islam' in some of the areas of their operations such as Kyazanga in Masaka District and Najjanankumbi, a Kampala suburb.

Moreover, in demanding the observance of the religio-political rights of Muslims, the Muslim community in Uganda has received inspiration and encouragement from Islamist activists in Sudan, Pakistan, Libya and Saudi Arabia in various ways. Sudan, in particular, has had a significant impact on the Tabliq Youths Movement. It is on record (Kayunga, 1993:40), for example, that when Dr Hasan al-Turabi, the architect of Islamic fundamentalism in Sudan visited Uganda in 1986, apart from holding discussions with several Muslim youth groups, he publicly called upon Muslims in Uganda 'to fight for their rights and identity'. This was at a party hosted for him by Dr Sulaiman Kiggundu, the then Governor of

Bank of Uganda. And, as Kayunga has argued (Kayunga, 1993: 41), the efforts of Sudan's Muslims to turn Sudan into an Islamic state, despite its large Christian and animist populations, has created confidence among the Muslim population in sub-Saharan countries with either a majority or a large minority of Muslims like Uganda, and gradually they too are demanding the observance of the rights of Muslims, including the establishment of an Islamic state.

Furthermore, it is a well-known fact that countries like Iran, Libya, Saudi Arabia and Sudan, would each very much like the Muslims in Uganda to embrace its brand of Islam and political ideology. It is hardly surprisingly, then, that during the 1987 UMSC General Assembly elections at Kibuli, Libya supported Sheikh Saad Luwemba both morally and materially. It is alleged, for instance, that in the run-up to the election (April 1987) Mr Mantuk of the Islamic Call Society of Libya told Makerere University Muslim students in the University Mosque that Libya's aim was to destroy utterly Saudi Arabia's influence in Uganda and that, if they supported Luwemba's candidature for the post of Mufti, Libya would give them everything they needed. The story of this election, which Sheikh Luwemba won, is now too well known (Kanyeihamba, 1993: 140-160) to merit further discussion here. Indeed, through their NGOs, countries like Libya, Sudan, Saudi Arabia and Iran are able to deploy sheikhs in Uganda to propagate their respective brands of Islam and political ideology. In fact, one of the reasons given by the Tabliq Youths Movement (*The New Vision*, August 23, 1990:9) for seizing the headquarters of the UMSC at Old Kampala in August 1990 and for attempting to oust Sheikh Rajab Kakooza's interim administration was that it had 'persistently continued to divide Ugandan Muslims along Saudi Arabian and Libyan lines'.

The propagation of the competing brands of Islam and ideologies in Uganda is backed up by financial and material assistance. Thus, for many years now, Libya, Sudan, Saudi Arabia and Iran have given, and continue to give, financial and material support to different groups and communities to facilitate the expansion of Qur'anic schools and mosques, thus enabling many more Muslims, who would otherwise remain unschooled, to improve their knowledge of Islamic studies. In addition, each of these countries has provided, and continues to provide, scholarships to deserving Muslim youths wishing to attend colleges and universities in the sponsoring countries. A good many of the respondents were of the view that the current upsurge in the demand for the rights of Muslims in Uganda is largely the result of the efforts of the beneficiaries of such scholarships who, on their return to the country after the completion of their studies, devote their entire working life to promoting Islamic culture since, as a rule, the government does not offer employment to graduates in Islamic studies.

There was a convergence of views among the respondents that the gist of the sermons by the graduates of foreign colleges and universities is that now is the time for Muslims in Uganda to fight for political power, which alone can facilitate the realisation of Islamic ideals in the country. It is worth noting too that this theme often attracts the attention of foreign dignitaries, particularly those from Iran, Libya, Saudi Arabia and Sudan who, when called upon to 'greet' the congregation, particularly during the *Jumu'a* Friday prayer, always endeavour to hammer it into the heads of their audiences. It can thus be concluded that it is the cumulative effect of education which has increased the Muslims' perception of their religio-political rights.

Today Islamic proselytisers vary widely in tone and emphasis; nonetheless, they tend to pay homage to the cause that toppled the Shah of Iran and inspired other Muslims to strive for a new cultural ascendancy. Iran's example, and in some cases its active aid, has re-emerged as a potent influence now that alienation from established regimes is deepening in step with economic hardships across the Islamic belt of Africa, the Middle East, South Asia, even in the Muslim desert reaches of western China.

Despite this glaring evidence linking the demand for Islamic religio-political rights in Uganda with foreign influence and involvement, Uganda's Muslims are shy to openly admit this connection. For example, 18 respondents, representing 26 percent, denied any connection between the current vigorous demand by Ugandan Muslims for the religio-political rights and the competing ideologies being propagated by the NGOs based in Libya, Sudan, Saudi Arabia and Iran. Rather, they were of the view that the current upsurge in the demand for the rights of Muslims in Uganda was a direct response to what they called 'savage repression of the Muslim population' by the NRM government. On the other hand 29 respondents, representing 41 percent, were mute on this research instrument, thus perhaps suggesting that they did not wish to commit themselves on the matter rather than being totally ignorant of it. However, responses from a respectable minority of 23 respondents, representing 33 percent, concurred that there was a direct link between the activities and operations of foreign-based Muslim NGOs and the current upsurge in demand for the rights of Muslims in the country.

Of course, this is hardly surprising. Because it is an inescapable religious duty for Muslims regardless of their nationality or domicile, to assist fellow Muslims, particularly those who are striving to end infidel rule and to establish an Islamic state. The Qur'an says (*Surah* 8:73):

> The Unbelievers are
> Protectors, one of another:
> Unless ye do this
> (Protect each other),
> There would be
> Tumult and oppression
> On earth, and great mischief.

The lesson to be learned from this verse is that, since evil concerts with evil, Muslims must draw together regardless of their nationality or country, not only by living in mutual harmony, but also by being ready at all times to provide material and any other form of assistance to fellow Muslims, particularly those who are suffering persecution, and are striving to end it. Otherwise, the world will be given over to aggression by unscrupulous people, and the good will fail in their duty to establish God's peace and to strengthen all the forces of truth and righteousness. It is little wonder, then, that foreign-based NGOs and foreign Islamic governments seem too ready to provide educational and material assistance to the Muslim population in Uganda. To do otherwise would amount to abdication of their religious duty. Indeed, the economic aid Uganda receives from Islamic countries like Libya and Saudi Arabia is regarded by these donor countries as the most valuable form of jihad, and its purpose is largely to further the frontiers of Islam by ending the alleged persecution of the Muslim community in Uganda. However, Muslims are also expected to give assistance to the poor, whether Muslim or not, and also to assist non-Muslims with whom they have signed an agreement and those who have given refuge to fellow Muslims.

True enough, the clamour for the religio-political rights of Muslims in Uganda is still in its embryonic stage. Nonetheless, a beginning has been made and the process is now unstoppable. However, with properly thought-out national policies, it can be guided, regulated and conditioned, say by the UMSC, not to gather along the way the virulent strains of radical Islamic fundamentalism that is the trademark of some of the Islamist groups in Egypt, Sudan, Pakistan, Libya, and Iran, which are the popular destinations for Ugandan youths in search of opportunities for higher Islamic education.

The Containment of Islamic Populism

The new trend the world over is for Muslims, particularly those imbued with radicalism, living under Westernised governments, such as that of Uganda, to clamour for the formation of their own political party with an Islamic platform to compete for state power. Because radical Islamic fundamentalists, in common with other Muslims, strongly believe that unless Muslims control state power, they cannot successfully protect Islam from the encroachment of Westernisation in today's world. Of course, it is politically sound in a democracy for a group of people, whether Muslim or not, who strongly feel that they have been marginalised and that their commonly shared interests are being trampled on by the government of the day, to form their own political organisation or party, in order to compete for state power, or at least, to increase their political influence with a view to disabusing the ruling party of the policies injurious to their interests.

Thus, it may not be prudent in today's era of political pluralism and good governance for the government to persist in its stubborn opposition to the formation of an Islamic political party since this would make a mockery of our young democracy. The NRM government's negative stance towards the formation of an Islamic party is borne out of its zealous opposition to 'religious fundamentalism of any faith that does not differentiate between the secular and the religious'. However, the government would be better advised to drop this opposition, since Islam does not make a distinction between secular and religious, and since the Muslim population in the country are most unlikely to forego this cardinal principle of their religion.

The biblical teaching (The Bible Societies, 1976: Mat. 22. 15-22): '... Well, then, pay the Emperor what belongs to the Emperor, and pay God what belongs to God', which is usually quoted by Western-oriented liberals to justify secularism, is in sharp contrast with Islamic teachings that emphasise that God is the sovereign of the state; that the Qur'an is the constitution of the state; and that every deed of Muslims individually and collectively must be inspired by the Qur'an. This makes Islam incompatible with secularism of the Western model and, from the Muslims' point of view, it makes the government's opposition to religious-political parties anti-Islam.

Indeed, there is nothing outrageous about the Muslims' demand to form their own political party with an Islamic platform. Indeed, religious-based political parties exist in some of the old democracies in Europe. Norton (Norton, 1994:50) has argued, for example, that democracy and Islam are not incompatible, since democracy is the demand of the people of the area to be included in the political system. 'So long as the Islamic fundamentalist movements are given no voice in politics,' Norton further contends, 'there can be no surprise that their rhetoric will be shrill and their stance uncompromising.' In contrast, well-designed strategies of political inclusion hold great promise for facilitating essential political change. The alternative to radicalism must be a party where Islamic fundamentalists can vent their grievances and participate in the political life of the country. The containment policy that is imposed from above by the government in the long run is not likely to succeed where other governments have woefully failed. The only meaningful and peaceful solution to the radicalisation of Islam in Uganda is the establishment of a legal Islamic party where the rights of minorities, political pluralism, and other essential issues become part of the party's constitution.

It is quite evident from the discussion in this book that radical Islamic fundamentalism is both a religious movement and an ideological movement which is borne out of socio-economic contradictions. It is imperative, therefore, that these should be addressed through democratic governance, transparency, and economic reconstruction of society if radical Islamic fundamentalism is to be curbed. And this is necessary for the good of society as a whole. Because radical Islamic fundamentalists (*The New Vision*, August 22, 1990:6) are intolerant of other religious groups including rival Islamic sects, this tends to breed propaganda wars that ultimately degenerate into open confrontations. For example, in 1990 a group of over 1000 members of the Tabliq Youths Movement seized the headquarters of the UMSC at Old Kampala and temporarily ousted Sheikh Rajab Kakooza's interim administration, accusing it of corruption, embezzlement, and of failing to extricate Islam from un-Islamic practices such as holding of last funeral rights and singing hymns at funerals.

Thus, if we are to curb the radicalisation of Islam in Uganda, we ought not only to address the symptoms but also the causes of radical Islamic fundamentalism since in a way it is a manifestation of both the economic and political maladies within society.

7

Which Way Forward?

Conclusions and Policy Suggestions

The conclusions given here are only tentative. More comprehensive research on the subject of this book is required before one can reach definitive conclusions on the issues relating to the observance of the rights of Muslims in Uganda. However, they provide the broad range of issues which should guide further research on the rights of Muslims in the country. And in the meantime they should form a basis for action by all those concerned with the development of Islam in Uganda.

Similarly, the policy suggestions that I have made here, which are largely drawn from the conclusions in question, are neither comprehensive nor definitive. But, until results of a more comprehensive research are availed to us, the present policy suggestions can be used as a basis for devising programmes to advance the cause of Islam in Uganda.

Conclusions

- The type of education given in the country's primary and secondary schools today is not befitting for Muslim children's spiritual and moral education.

- Speaking generally, the acquisition of Islamic education including Arabic, improves the Muslims' perception of their religio-political rights as well as enhancing their spirituality, since, it is through reading the Arabic Quar'an that a Muslim can be expected to understand the reality of its inimitability and to discover the secret of its eloquence. Moreover, the Arabic language provides the basis for a Muslim to interpret the Qur'an and thus be able to apply its teachings to his daily life.

- Graduates of foreign colleges and universities, who have been exposed to virulent strains of Islamism and various Islamic theological schools of thought in these foreign institutions, are largely responsible for religious diversities and doctrinal disagreements among Muslims in Uganda.

- The demand for a non-working Friday by some Muslim groups, on the grounds that this would give Muslims adequate time to attend the *Jumu'a* prayer, arises very largely out of ignorance of the Qur'anic injunctions on the *Jumu'a* prayer.

- Even though there have not been obvious acts of oppression by the Movement government directed specifically at Muslims as a religious group, nevertheless, many Muslims strongly believe that, since the overthrow of Idi Amin's regime in 1979, they have been oppressed and marginalised by successive Uganda governments.

- Today's Muslims' increased religious consciousness has whetted their desire for the introduction of Islamic governance thus making them less disposed to vote for candidates of political organisations without an Islamic platform in future national elections.

- The Movement government's alleged involvement in the election of Muslim leaders, particularly the Mufti, whether directly or indirectly, is loathed by a majority of Muslims, who regard it as manipulation of the electoral process to ensure that the elections produce spineless leaders who are supportive of government policies at the expense of Muslims' interests.

- A good many Ugandan Muslims are not very knowledgeable about the sharia, and as a consequence they, knowingly or unknowingly, tend to ignore some of its most important injunctions such as the payment of *zakat* which, even though it is the third pillar of Islam, is generally not paid by a good many of those liable to pay it.

- Government functionaries quite often act with no regard to Muslims' sensitivities. Take, for example, the practice by the Uganda Police Force and the Ministry of Justice of bringing Muslims suspected of committing some crimes before Magistrates' courts on Friday afternoon, when they should be attending the *Jumu'a* prayer. For Muslims, this practice is very humiliating indeed.

Policy Suggestions

- Since Muslims truly believe that the Qur'an is a revealed book and infallible, and since any contrary view would attract swift and drastic response in the form of a jihad of the sword, it is recommended that the UMSC should be mandated to set professional standards for training Imams and others wishing to preach in mosques in Uganda. (The current (2003) leadership of the UMSC does not consider such a scenario appropriate at the present level of Islamic development in Uganda, however.) The UMSC might emulate the example of some Muslim states which issue certificates of competence to people wishing to preach in mosques as a career. In this regard, the UMSC deserves massive financial support from donors and Muslim NGOs so that it can embark on an aggressive training programme for the Imams and Sheikhs that are needed to advance Islam in Uganda.

- Since our constitution (1995) guarantees freedom of religion, it is recommended that, as much as possible, the government should endeavour not to enact laws which directly or indirectly contravene the spirit and principles of Islamic law. It is further recommended that the Ministry of Justice and Constitutional Affairs should establish a Department of Sharia Affairs which would be charged with the responsibility of advising the government on the compatibility or otherwise of national laws and the sharia.

- Since Muslims have a religious obligation to attend the *Jumu'a* prayer on Friday at noon, it is recommended that government-aided schools, colleges, and universities which are attended by Muslims, should not schedule regular lessons between 12.00 and 2.00 p.m. on Fridays so as to enable Muslim students to attend the *Jumu'a* prayer. It is further recommended that the government should grant its Muslim employees an extended lunch break on Friday to enable them to attend the *Jumu'a* prayer.

- Since Muslims are required to pray five times a day and at specific times, and since the 1995 Constitution of Uganda guarantees freedom of worship, it is recommended that the government should actively encourage employers of labour and educational institutions to provide places of worship for their Muslim clientele.

- Since Muslims require a unique type of education, including a knowledge of the Arabic language to practise their religion properly, it is hereby recommended that the government should actively encourage and financially support the teaching of Islamic studies in primary and secondary schools attended by Muslims. It is further recommended that Qur'anic studies and Arabic should be included in the official syllabuses of primary and secondary schools and tertiary institutions and universities and made compulsory subjects for Muslim students. Indeed, not only are Muslims expected to read the Arabic text of the Qur'an but also to teach it to others. This is in accordance with what Prophet Muhammad said (Islamic Researches, 1992: that 'The best among you is he who learned the Qur'an and then taught it'. This shows the extent to which Muslims are duty-bound to read the Qur'an, preferably the Arabic text.

- Since there seems to be a correlation between one's level of education, particularly Islamic education, and one's perception of the religio-political rights of Muslims, it is recommended that the government should financially support the UMSC to establish a National College of Higher Islamic Education to train Imams, Arabists and other experts in Islamic studies. Not only would this promote better understanding of Islam, which would be good for the country since Islamic radicalism tends to thrive on ignorance, but would also remove the necessity for Ugandan Muslim youths to be lured to seek educational opportunities in foreign countries where they are likely to be exposed to virulent strains of Islamic radicalism. Furthermore, such training would produce young Sheikhs who could be employed elsewhere instead of solely seeking employment in Islamic establishments. This would reduce unemployment among graduates in Islamic studies which sometimes leads to squabbles between the Imams and unemployed graduate youths about who should control their local mosque.

Disturbing trends in Muslim nations, e.g. Algeria, Afghanistan, and Indonesia, such as the rise in Islamic extremism, provide the public impetus for giving Muslim youths a good quality education (good for purpose). This is because, more often than not, Islamic extremism (Usman, 1987:21-23) is concomitant of the manipulation of Muslims, particularly the deprived youths, by crafty *ulama* or politicians who seek to create personal religious constituencies to increase their power and wealth by using Islam. And if we take manipulation to mean control of somebody skilfully or craftily, especially by using unfair methods without the person being manipulated being aware that some form of control was being exercised over him, the essential precondition for manipulation is ignorance on the part of the person being manipulated. Hence, a good quality Islamic higher education, which would enable Muslim youths, both male and female, to earn their livelihoods and to be self-reliant, to grasp the teachings of the Qur'an, and to be God-fearing, is the only bulwark against radicalisation of Islam in Uganda.

For instance, while opening the World Conference of Islamic Scholars in Kuala Lumpur on 10 July 2003 the then Malaysian Prime Minister, Dr Mahathir Mohamad, observed that Muslim countries had themselves to blame for being humiliated by the US-led fight against terrorism since, from his point of view, false interpretation of the Qur'an and the Muslim countries' failure to keep pace with modern developments had led to a decline of Islamic civilisation. He then exhorted the conference that the solution to these twin problems was for the Muslim countries to take immediate action against 'extreme interpretation of Islamic teachings', which in his view, 'weakens Muslim nations for the benefits of foreign powers'. 'The prime duty of the Islamic scholars', according to Dr Mohamad, was 'to inform the *Ummah* about the possible implications of such interpretations' and that 'the information can be through formal or non-formal education'. 'This,' in his view, 'was because extremist groups were banking on people's ignorance about the true teachings of Islam'. He further told the conference that it was essential for Muslim countries to unite and to master science and technology if they were to stand up to their oppressors and to restore Islamic civilisation to its past glory. (Website. M. Mohamad, Speeches & Resolution. Retrieved on 13 July 2003 from the World Wide Web.)

For his part, Professor A.A. Mohammad Ibrahim of the Khartoum International Institute of Arabic Language told the same Conference that Islamic universities such as Egypt's al-Azhar University and the International Islamic University of Malaysia – he might have added the IUIU – had an important role to play in shaping the future graduates of the Islamic world that the conference expected to be free of Islamic fanaticism. (Website. Ibrahim, Speeches & Resolution. Retrieved on 13 July 2003 from the World Wide Web.) Obviously, Professor Ibrahim's claim here strengthens the case for the establishment of a national institution for higher Islamic education in Uganda that could build a 'stream of Islamic knowledge' that would pave the way for the advancement of the Muslims in this era of globalisation.

Indeed in the opinion of Sheikh Husamuddin al-Qaraqiraah (website. Speeches & Resolution; Retrieved on 13 July 2003 from the World Wide Web), who addressed the World Conference of Islamic Scholars on the question of the development of extremist ideology and its effects on the Islamic civilisation, argued that the best way or method to extirpate Islamic extremism is to train Muslim preachers so that they are armed with sound knowledge and ready with proofs and evidence to expose the extremists to the world so as to prevent them from speaking deceitfully in the name of Islam. Thus in the fight against Islamic extremism, which Sheikh al-Qaraqirah describes as 'a scientific war', the scholars and sheikhs are the first and strongest line of defence who should take pre-emptive actions against the designs of the extremists to prevent them from fortifying their position in society.

- Since Muslims regard the election of their leaders, particularly the Mufti (one appointed, or at least competent, to give a formal legal opinion (*fatwa*, plural *fatawa*), as a form of worship, and since many Muslims regard government involvement in such elections as direct interference with their freedom of worship, it is recommended that in future the government should restrict its role in these elections to financial support and ensuring security of the participants in the elections. Even if the government were to deploy its Muslim functionaries to plan and conduct elections for Muslim leaders, it would not be enough to satisfy Muslim skeptics of the government's good intentions since the government functionaries so deployed might be seen as government agents.

- Since paying *zakat* is an obligation for Muslims that are blessed with wealth, and since detailed rules are laid down in the texts (e.g. Malik, 1982:121-35) as to the property on which *zakat* is to be levied, the percentage payable, and also regarding the purpose to which the proceeds are to be dedicated, and since a good many of the Ugandan Muslims are not very knowledgeable about these rules, it might be a good idea if the UMSC could double its efforts to educate Muslims on matters pertaining to *zakat* through seminars, conferences, sermons in mosques, use of television, radio, and relevant literature. Indeed the UMSC has plans to solicit money from donor countries and NGOs and to distribute it to the districts to support educational activities in these districts. This is a good idea which should be supported by all men of good will for the sake of advancing Islam in Uganda.

- The government should consider opening up a window of opportunity for Islamic banking in the country's banking system to ensure that *zakat* funds are not subjected to non-Islamic financial rules and regulations. We should take a leaf out of Britain's book where some banks, e.g. Lloyds TSB Bank, now operate Islamic accounts in a sharia-compliant way.

Bibliography

Abdurrahman, M. and Peter Canhan, 1978. *The Ink of the Scholar: The Islamic Tradition of Education in Nigeria*, Lagos, Macmillan, Nigeria Ltd.

Abraham, A.J., 1989. *Khoumani and Islamic Fundamentalism : Contributions of Islamic Sciences to Modern Civilisation*, 2nd edn. N.P. Cloverdale Library.

Adamu, Mahdi, 2002. 'Islamisation of Knowledge in a Multi-Religious Society', *Islamic University Journal*, the IUIU, vol. 2, No. 2, p.1-6.

Al-Azm, S., 1993. 'Islamic Fundamentalism Reconsidered: A Critical Outline of Problems, Ideas, and Approaches', *South Asia Bulletin*, vol. 13, Nos. 1 and 2, p.93-131.

Al-Azmi, T.H., 1994. 'Religions, Identity, and State in Modern Islam', *Muslim World*, vol. 84, Nos. 3 and 4, p.334-341.

Ali, M. Cheragh. 1984. *A Critical Exposition of the Popular Jihad*, Delhi, Idarah-i Adabiyat-i, Delli.

Ali, S.A., 1987. 'Islam and Modern Education', *Muslim Education Quarterly*, vol. 4, No. 3, p.36-44.

Ali, Y.A., 1973. *The Glorious Kur'an, Translation and Commentary*, Tripoli, the Call of Islam Society.

Al-Qaraqirah, H., July 10-12, 2003. Web site. 'Speeches & Resolution': *http://www.bernama.com/events/ulama/rspeech.shtml?speech/se2002-1a*

Al-Turabi, Hassan, 1992. 'The Islamic Awakening's Second Wave', *New Perspectives Quarterly*, vol. 9, (Summer) pp.52-55

Anawati, G., 1974. 'Philosophy, Theology and Mysticism', in Joseph Schacht (ed.) *The Legacy of Islam*, Oxford, Oxford University Press, pp.350-358.

Anderson, J.H.D., 1970. *Islamic Law in Africa*, New Impression, London, Frank Cass and Co. Ltd.

Anderson, L., 1987. 'The State in the Middle East and North Africa', *Comparative Politics*, vol. 20, No. 1 p.1-18.

Antoun, Richard, and M.E. Hegland, (eds.), 1987. *Religious Resurgence: Contemporary Cases in Islam, Christianity, and Judaism*. Syracuse: Syracuse University Press.

Arjomand, S.Amir (ed.), 1988. *Authority and Political Culture in Shi'ism*, Albany, State University of New York Press.

Azzam, Salam, 1982. *Islam and Contemporary Society*, London, Longman.

Beedham, B., 1944. 'A Survey of Islam', *The Economist*, August 6th p.1-18.

Bjorkman, W.J. (ed.), 1988. *Fundamentalism, Revivalists and Violence in South Asia*, Delhi, Manohar.

Dessouki, Ali E. Hillal, 'The Islamic Resurgence', in Ali E.H. Dessouki (ed.), 1982. *Islamic Resurgence in the Arab World*, New York, Praeger. pp.9-23.

El-Mokhtar, Ould Bah M. tr. from Arabic by A. El-Hakhouni, 1998. *Islamic Education Between Tradition and Modernity*, Publication of the Islamic Educational, Scientific and Cultural Organisation.

Esposito, John L., 1992. *The Islamic Threat: Myth or Reality?*, New York, Oxford University Press.

Fafunwa, A.B., 1974. *History of Education in Nigeria*, London, George Allen & Unwin.

Filali-Ansari, A., 1996. 'Islam and Liberal Democracy: the Challenge of Secularization,' *Journal of Democracy*, vol. 7, No. 2, p.76-80.

Funabashi, Yochi, 1992. 'Globalize Asia,' *New Perspective Quarterly*, vol. 9 (winter). pp.23-24

Flores, A., 1993. 'Secularism, Integralism and Political Islam,' *Middle East Report*, No. 183, p.32-38.

Gove, P.B., et al. (eds)., 1986. *Webster's Third New International Dictionary of the English Language, Unabridged.* Springfield, Merrian-Webster Inc. Publishers.

Hamdi, M.E., 1996. 'Islam and Liberal Democracy : the Limits of the Western Model', *Journal of Democracy*, vol. 7, No.2, p.81-85.

Harrison, L.E. and S.P. Huntington, (eds.), 2000. *Culture Matters: How Values Shape Human Progress*, New York, Basic Books.

Hiro, D., 1989. *Holy Wars: The Rise of Islamic Fundamentalism*, New York, Routledge.

Hiskett, M., 1984. *The Development of Islam in West Africa*, London, Longman.

Holger, B.H. and M. Twaddle (eds.), 1995. *Religion and Politics in East Africa*, London, James Currey.

Hovsepian, N., 1995. 'Competing Identities in the Arab World', *Journal of International Affairs*, vol. 49, pp.1-24.

Huntington, S.P., 1996. *'The Clash of Civilisations and the Remaking of World Order*, New York, Simon & Schuster.

Huntington, S., 1993. 'The Clash of Civilisations', *Foreign Affairs*, vol. 72, No.3, pp.22-49.

Huntington, S.P., 1968. *Political Order in Changing Societies*, New Haven and London, Yale University Press.

Ibrahim, A.A.M. July 10-12, 2003. Website. 'Speeches & Resolution': Retrieved 13 July 2003 from the World Wide

Web: *htt://www.bernama.com.my/events/oicsummit/oicbasic/ news.open.php? cat=bI & id =3694*

Ibrahim, A.B., 1995. 'Intellectual Origins of Islamic Resurgence in the Modern Arab World: the Contemporary Academic Debate', *Islamic Studies* (Islamabad), vol. 34, No. 2, pp.43-46.

Iqbal, Munamar (ed.), 1988. *Distributive Justice and Need Fulfilment in an Islamic Economy*, 2nd edn., Leicester, The Islamic Foundation.

Kanyeihamba, G.W., 1998. *Reflections on the Muslim Leadership Question in Uganda*, Kampala Fountain Publishers Ltd.

Karugire, S.R., 1980. *A Political History of Uganda*, Nairobi, Heinemann Educational Books.

Kasozi, Abdu B., 1994. *The Social Origins of Violence in Uganda 1964 -1983*, Montreal & Kingston, McGill-Queen's University Press.

Kasozi, Abdu B., 1986. *The Spread of Islam in Uganda*, Nairobi, Oxford University Press.

Kasozi, I. Immam, 2004. 'The Domestic Relations Bill and Sharia', *The 17th Annual Ramadhan Convention*, the IUIU, Mbale, 28-31.

Kasumba, Yusuf, 1995. 'The Development of Islam in Uganda;1962-1992: with Particular Reference to Religio-Political Factionalism'; M.A. Thesis, Makerere University.

Kayunga, S.S., 1993. *Islamic Fundamentalism in Uganda: A Case Study of the Tabliq Youth Movement*, Kampala, Centre for Basic Research.

Kramer, G., 1993. 'Islamic Notions of Democracy', *Middle East Report*, 23, No. 183, p.2-8.

Lewis, B., 1993. 'Islam and Liberal Democracy,' *Atlantic Monthly*, 271, p.89-98.

Malik, Imam, 1982. *Al-Muwatta*, tr. by Aisha A. At-Tarjumana, and Yaqub Johnson, Norwich, Diwan Press.

Malik, J. Website. 'Making Sense of Islamic Fundamentalism', Retrieved on 15 May 2001 from the World Wide Web: http://www.isim.nl/newletter/1/research/01 AD30.html.

Mamdani, Mahmood, 2004. *Good Muslim, Bad Muslim: America, the Cold War, and the Roots of Terror*. Kampala, Fountain Publishers.

Marty, Martin E. and R.S. Appleby, (eds.),1993. *Fundamentalism and Society*, Chicago, University of Chicago Press.

Menashri, D. (ed.), 1990. *The Iranian Revolution and the Muslim World*, Boulder, Colo. Westview Press.

Mika'ilu, A.S., 2002. 'Problems of Implementing Islamisation of Knowledge Programme in a Conventional University', *Islamic University Journal*, the IUIU, vol.2, No. 2, p.7-18.

Miller, J., 1993. 'The Challenge of Radical Islam', *Foreign Affairs*, vol. 72, No. 2, p.43-55.

Mohamad, M., July 10-12, 2003. Web site. 'Speeches & Resolution': Retrieved on 13 July 2003 from the World Wide Web: htt//www.bernama.com.my/bernama/v3/newsphp?id =3818; and http://www.bernama.com/events/ulama/rspeech.shtml?speech/sehamid-I.

Moussalli, A.S., 1999. *Moderate and Radical Islamic Fundamentalism: The Quest for Modernity, Legitimacy,* and *the Islamic State*, Gainesville, University Press of Florida.

Norton, A.R., 1994. 'Inclusion Can Deflate Islamic Populism', *New Perspective Quarterly*; vol. 10, No.3, p.50.

Parsa, Misagh, 1989. *Social Origins of the Iranian Revolution*, London, Rutgers University Press.

Peters, R., 1995. *Jihad in Classical and Modern Islam*, Princeton, Princeton University Press.

Bibliography 133

Peters, R., 2003. *Islamic Criminal Law in Nigeria*, Ibadan, Spectrum Books Ltd.

Porteous, J. 'The Islamisation of Modernity', *Middle East*, 220, p.19-22.

Rogers, M.B., 1990. *Cold Anger: A Study of Faith and Power Politics*, Denton, University of North Texas Press.

Rashid, Ahmed, 2001. *Taliban: The Story of the Afghan Warlords*, London, Pan Books.

Sen, Amartya, 1999. *Development as Freedom*, New York, Anchor Books.

Siddiqi, M. 1993. *Modern Reformist Thought in the Muslim World*, Delhi, Adam Publishers.

Stone, Martin, 1993. *The Agony of Algeria*, New York, Columbia University Press.

Sulaiman, Ibrahim, January 3, 1988. 'Muslim as a Ruler', *Sunday New Nigerian*, Kaduna, New Nigerian corporation, p.2-3 and 5.

The Bible Societies, 1976. *Good News Bible*, Collins & Glasgow.

The International Institute of Islamic Thought, 1989. *Toward Islamisation of Disciplines*, Herndon.

The Monitor Newspaper, Kampala, The Monitor Publications Ltd., January 11, 18 and 19, 1998; March 3, 1999; and September 5, 2000.

The New Vision, Kampala, The New Vision Printing and Publishing Corporation, May 24, 2000.

The Presidency of Islamic Researches (eds.), 1999. *The Holy Qur'an : English Translation of the Meanings and Commentary*, Medina, King Fahd Holy Qur'an Printing Complex. (The Original text was translated by Abdallah Yusuf Ali.)

Tibenderana, P.K., 2003. *Education and Cultural Change in Northern Nigeria 1906-1966: A Study in the Creation of a Dependent Culture*, Kampala, Fountain Publishers Ltd.

Tiberondwa, Ado, 1998. *Missionary Teachers as Agents of Colonialism in Uganda*, Kampala, Fountain Publishers.

Tomodonfar, M., 1989. *The Islamic Polity and Political Leadership: Fundamentalism, Sectarianism, and Pragmatism*, Boulder, Colo: Westview Press.

The Shariat Newsletter, Kampala, Publisher, August 8-14, 1995.

Tiji-Farouki, S., 1995. 'Islamic State-Theories and Contemporary Realities'. In Siodahamed, A.S. and A. Ehteshemi (eds.), *Islamic Fundamentalism*, Boulder, Colo. Westview Press.

Uganda Government, 2002. *Political Parties and Organisations Act*, Entebbe, 2002.

Uganda Bureau of Statistics, 2005. *The 2002 Uganda Population and Housing Census*, Kampala, Uganda Bureau of Statistics.

Usman, B.Y., 1987. *The Manipulation of Religion in Nigeria 1977-1987*. Kaduna, Vanguard Publishers Ltd.

Watt, W.M. 1962. Islamic Surveys: *Islamic Philosophy and Theology*, Edinburgh, Edinburgh University Press.

Index

Ahmadiya Muslims (Ug.) 9
Amin, Idi 8; his regime; see also administration 10, 74, 100, 121
Anglo-Buganda Agreement 1900 xviii
Baganda Muslim refugees 5, 7
British colonial administration xvii, 7, 99
Buddhism 2
Christian(s) xxii, 2, 39, 52, 70, 83, 109; –culture 80; – missionaries xvii; – schools 83.
Democratic Party (Ug.) ixi, 106, 108
Domestic Relations Bills of 1989 and 2003 89-94
East African coast xvii, 5
Exertion 18-19. See also Jihad
Fundamentalism(st) xx, 3; Islamic – xxi, 19-27, 95, 101, 117; – movements 2, 3, 5, 118; phenomenon of Islamic – 40-66, 80
Hajj 46 -49
Hinduism 2,5
Islam xvii, xxi, xxiii, 2, 3, 5, 7, 15, 16, 19, 30, 39, 72, 82, 117; and politics 30-37; divorce in – 62-66; growing of – in Ug. 6; history of – in Ug. 6-11; marriage in – 61, 85; political state of – 27-37; polygamy in 61-62, 67; resurgence of – 1,

2; revolution and – 24; rule of – 27; sciences of tradition xxiii; understanding of – 15-26
Islamic: aspects 15; – call 31-32; – culture and civilisation 82, 95, 109, 125; – education 57-60, 72, 81, 120, 123, 125; law (see also sharia) xxii, 17, 23, 32, 35, 41-42, 49, 70, 96; – principles 81, 122; – religious education 82, 84 – resurgence 95-98, 106, 108, 110
Islamic government 28, 87; see also Il-Hukuma al-Islamiyya
Islamic state(s) 21-22, 26-27, 29, 32-33, 37, 38, 71, 144; aim of – 40; and shura 27-30, 31; conceptualisation of an – 27-37; religio-political rights of Muslims under an – 38-66, 67, 120; sovereignity in – 35
Islamic University in Uganda (IUIU) xxv, xxvi, 8, 79 - 80
Islamisation 3; – of knowledge 79, 80, 96
Jihad of the sword 49-54, 73-74, 122
Kibirige Mayanja, Muhammad 112
Legacy of colonial education in Ug. 80-85;
Muhammad, Prophet 15, 21, 22, 35, 46, 56, 60, 78, 87, 123
Meseveni, Yoweri Kaguta (pres. Ug.) 110

Muslim(s) xvii, xxii; – community in Ug. 11,16, 35, 40, 52, 59, 74, 81, 109; education of – in Uganda xix, xx 5, 7, 8; legal system of – in Uganda 70; education of– in Uganda 78-80; – marriages 85, 86, 90, 93; non-governmental organisations of – 10, 102, 116, 122; religio-political rights of – xviii, xix, 13, 15, 99, 100; rights of – in Ug. xx, xxiii 65-94, 116; Sunni in Ug.; traders 7, 9, 13, 14, 39;

Muslim population in Uganda 68, 81, 95, 100, 111, 112; right of – to be ruled by a Muslim 68-69; right of – to be ruled in accordance with the sharia 69-71

Muslim world 22, 46, 96

National Resistance Movement (NRM) 10, 11, 74, 102, 105, 110, 111, 116

Political Parties and Organisations Act 2002 105, 109

Protestants in Uganda 5, 6, 105

Ramadhan 45-46

Religion(ous); and cultural identity 23, 95; diversities and doctrinal disagreements 8; groups 8, 4; resurgence 3, 4

Revolution and Islam 24

Roman Catholics in Ug. 5,6,105

Uganda Islamic Revolutionary Party (UIRP) 104, 105, 109

Uganda Muslim Supreme Council (UMSC) xxv, 8, 9, 11, 93, 101, 106, 114, 117, 122, 124, 127

Uganda Muslim youth Assembly (UMYA) 91, 92, 93

Uganda Peoples Congress (UPC) 104, 106, 108

Uganda's Independence, October 1962 xviii, 83

Zakat funds 54-57, 74; – in Uganda 75-76, 121, 126, 127

www.ingramcontent.com/pod-product-compliance
Lightning Source LLC
Chambersburg PA
CBHW021408290426
44108CB00010B/438